MW01398808

A WORK IN PROGRESS
PORTRAIT OF THE UNIVERSITY OF MICHIGAN–FLINT

Robert W. Heywood

copyright © 1996, The Regents of the University of Michigan
Published by the University of Michigan–Flint
Office of the Chancellor
303 East Kearsley Street
Flint, Michigan 48503-2186

All rights reserved. No part of this publication may be reproduced or transmitted in any form or by any means, electronic or mechanical, including photocopying, recording, or by any information storage and retrieval system, without permission in writing from The University of Michigan–Flint.

Printed and bound in the United States of America
Library of Congress Number 96-06090

ISBN 0-9653426-0-3

Table of Contents

Introduction i
The Place — Flint, Michigan 1
The Beginning 2
The College and Cultural Center 4
The First Metamorphosis — The Four-Year Flint College 4
Trouble with the State Board of Education 5
Growing Pains 6
The "Pioneer" Generation 7
The *Dorr Report* — The first of the Founding Documents 9
The College Community — A Sense of Family 13
Where's the Library? 14
General Education Requirements: The Bett Plan 16
Space Problems 18
Living in the Flint Area 18
Flint College Students — Understanding Who They Really Were! A Faculty View 22
The Second Metamorphosis: From College to Regional University Campus 26
Shifting Gears — A Decade of Fulfillment and Promise 32
The Riverfront Campus 36
Academic Planning for a Regional Campus 39
The Honors Program 41
Other Changes 43
The 5.09 Matter 43
Graduate Teaching Assistants and Contingency Faculty 44
Shared Governance 45
A Sense of Community 48
The Academic Community in Search of Itself: The 1980s 54
The Jones Era 55
Minority Issues: A Focus on Diversity 55
An Administrative Response 59
Problems Emerge 60
The Flint Campus Issue 60
And, On Another Front, Some Strategic Planning 62
The Academic Advising Center 65
To Organize or Not? Collective Bargaining and a Faculty Union 66
Campus Expansion: The Thompson Library and the University Pavilion 72
Changing the Face of the Fortress 74
The University Pavilion 74
The Women's Center 75
A Multiple Unit Campus 76
The Passing Present 79
The Fourth Chancellor 80
The Kugler Academic Plan 82
Whither Quality? 85
Whither Liberal Education? 87
The Arts 89
Conclusion and Comment 90
Some New Thinking 90
About Community Expectations 92
The Corporate Model — Running it like a Business? 94
Room for Optimism 96

Introduction

The content and scope of this brief book are not quite as originally intended. What I anticipated at the outset, when this was all in a more conceptual stage, was "The Story of The University of Michigan–Flint." It was to be a story recounting a bit of campus history, a story that would focus on the experiences and perceptions of those people who, over the years, have been associated either with the early Flint College or, since 1973, with The University of Michigan–Flint. As it turns out, this is not altogether what you will find here.

If there has been default in this regard, in another there has not. It was not intended that "a history" be written. While these pages suggest a generally historical approach, they do not constitute a history. While others might attempt a more detailed and exhaustive history, a comprehensive historical overview can be found in Professor Robert G. Schafer's "A History of The University of Michigan–Flint," which was published in 1990 by the Genesee Historical Collections Center in cooperation with the Genesee County Historical Society. There is also the still useful and insightful study by Professor Edward T. Calver, "A History of the Flint College" (1971). Writing history requires a scope of careful and systematic research and of critical analysis not found in the following essay.

With all of these disclaimers, what do we have here? As the title suggests, this book constitutes a "portrait" of a college turned regional university campus in sustained transition, thus the phrase "a work in progress." It is a portrait of a work in progress!

Why a portrait? A portrait allows for more interpretive comment than would be appropriate in a history. A portrait does not pretend to embrace all discernible features; it can be selective. It allows one to be more personal. At the same time, a portrait should be both credible and lead the reader to some new and meaningful insights, perhaps to a better understanding, in this case about the development of an institution in a set of unique circumstances. And while the reader may not agree with every feature of the interpretation, I trust that the larger narrative will be perceived as fair and balanced.

If this were set forth as "the story" of The University of Michigan–Flint, its scope would have to be much more comprehensive than it is. There are very important pieces in this campus story which are not given sufficient attention for it to pretend to be comprehensive. This book, then, should not be read either as "a history" or as "the story" of The University of Michigan - Flint. As "a portrait" it is episodic, thematic, and topical. It is also selective. Students, staff, and alumni — and numbers of administrators — receive less attention than the central focus of this portrait: the academic community. The academic community is understood to mean faculty and students engaged in learning, with the bedrock of that community being the faculty. Everything else certainly is important and consequential, but with the exception of some influential administrators it is peripheral to what this portrait attempts to convey.

The perspective found here is that of the faculty, and even then certainly not all of the faculty. In general terms it represents (beyond the views of the author) the opinions and comments of about one hundred past and present faculty and about a score of past and present staff. Many of those comments have been filtered through the mind and word processor of the author. There is some attribution but in many cases questions to faculty and staff colleagues were met with "Don't quote me, but . . ." Requests for anonymity have been respected, not that anything here might be regarded as outrageous or dangerously subversive. In many instances numbers of faculty expressed much the same view on an issue. Only in a few instances, however, is it suggested that a view or opinion was demonstrably that of the larger number, perhaps of a majority. No such measure of faculty opinion was taken on any issue. In any event, it would indeed be walking on very thin ice to suggest anything other than the fact that most often there were nearly the number of opinions on some matters as there were faculty to express them.

Additional portraits or perspectives on the story of The University of Michigan–Flint need to be written. This is certainly not the only one that might represent the memories and views of a significant number of faculty. A sequel to this "portrait" is being prepared by Alice Garrison, a staff member at the campus public television station, WFUM/TV28. Alice's focus will be on the perceptions and experiences of University of Michigan–Flint staff members. Also needed is a narrative that would convey the experiences, expectations, frustrations, and successes of current students and of some 17,000 alumni. A large number of those, nearly 12,000, continue to live in the Flint area or elsewhere in east central Michigan. That, too, would be a very useful and illuminating undertaking.

There are certain suppositions from which this whole project proceeded. As will be evident, the University of Michigan association — the connection with the mother campus in Ann Arbor — is regarded throughout as fundamental, as overriding, as all-important. A portrait of something other than The University of Michigan Flint College and something other than The University of Michigan–Flint would be profoundly different. A "University of Flint," without doubt, would have been an altogether different institution. At the very least the overwhelming number of Flint faculty would have sought appointments elsewhere had there not been the University of Michigan affiliation. Other concerns and issues, as those have surfaced in the past 40 years, pale by comparison with this fundamental point.

I have also assumed that it has been people more than the circumstances in which the campus has found itself over the course of these past four decades that have been most important in shaping what the institution has been and the directions in which it appears to be moving.

This portrait quite intentionally centers on those who were more immediately engaged in the larger life of the institution. We need to remember something here. Many of the faculty, the majority most of the time, were more preoccupied with departmental and personal professional concerns than with campus matters. Others were (and are) temperamentally uninterested in those larger issues and, unless their immediate interests were clearly in jeopardy, were inclined to "leave the running of the campus to those administrators hired for that reason" — a common jibe from faculty whose colleagues, in their view, were unwisely expending their energies in matters beyond their proper purview.

So why should we be concerned with the actions and opinions of those faculty who are variously perceived as (at best) the group constructively engaged in concern for the larger life of the academic community, the institution as a whole — or (at worst) dissidents and malcontents whose involvement was questionably constructive and of doubtful influence? The reason is two-fold. First, it is the people who have been deeply and consistently engaged in the larger life of the academic community who helped bring about change, set the tone, and influence direction. This is a diverse group. It includes faculty, certain administrators, on occasion some of the staff, and, we like to think, some of the more outspoken students. Second, it is the very presence of "dissidents," those prepared to take issue with administrative policy and the prevailing wisdom, who make possible a meaningful system of shared governance in which both administrators and faculty have important roles. It is, of course, fundamentally the point that the academic community is defined by faculty and students engaged in learning. That is a premise found throughout these pages. The larger issues and policy arena, however, provide the supportive framework — the resource environment — in which learning acquires dimension and meaning.

The brush stroke, then, is broad. It is institutional. The consequence, quite deliberately, is that one finds rather little here about individual faculty or individual departments except when some brief descriptive comment or, on occasion, an anecdote might shed light on the larger issues or illustrate a more general point about the campus at that particular time. Clearly, too, the task of describing the professional lives and accomplishments of hundreds of faculty, and of more than fifty academic programs, is well beyond the scope of this far more modest effort.

I did not initially intend to devote as much comment to deans and chancellors as you will find here. In fact, some brief thought was given to the idea that administrators should be generally ignored. This was to be about faculty and the academic experience at the Flint Campus of The University of Michigan. It still has that focus, at its core, though not many of these pages were written before the obvious became clear. Chancellors, deans, and other administrators have an ever-present and overriding role in making decisions about resources and, very clearly, a pivotal role in setting the tone for all dimensions of campus life. One cannot escape them. In a very real sense, administrators constitute a necessary added dimension to the academic community. My working premise, however, is that faculty and students, the learning community, are the very heart and soul of that community. It was in that frame of mind that I solicited comments and opinions from both faculty and staff colleagues.

Neither did I anticipate that a succession of planning documents over nearly forty years would assume such pivotal consequence in the writing of this portrait. It was not always what those five basic documents proposed that was important or that provided real insight as to what was going on. Sometimes it was what was not said and what subsequently failed to occur, that was more revealing about the realities of the moment and the directions in which the campus appeared to be moving. Either way, looking at both the rhetoric and the consequences of those planning exercises provided another dimension, beyond the simplest one of chronology and augmented numbers and size, to the "work in progress," a portrait of The University of Michigan–Flint.

The debts I have accumulated in the preparation of this "portrait" are many. In the first instance, it was Alice Garrison at WFUM/TV28 whose idea it was to write the story of The University of Michigan–Flint. She believed this might be a significant way in which the 40th anniversary of the University's Flint Campus could be commemorated. Her inspiration and many hours of conversation provided the point of departure for my efforts. I also am indebted to those many faculty and staff colleagues, both past and present, whose recollections and opinions have given this portrait dimension and content.

Most especially I want to thank Grant Burns, a librarian at the Thompson Library of The University of Michigan–Flint, and Professor Leslie Moch at Michigan State University, for their indispensable help with the text. Grant Burns, with his red pen, reminded me of the time consuming effort that good writing requires. I owe him a considerable debt for both the time and talent he brought to the task of helping me improve some very rough drafts. My thanks also to Professor Anita Barry of the English Department for her comments on an early draft; and to my ever-patient wife Irene who listened to interminable musings about what should find its way into this book, and whose comments on the draft helped make the text more clear. To all of those who read the early drafts and encouraged me to continue with the project, I am grateful. I found their criticisms and comments of great value. Any factual errors, of course, I will have to claim for myself.

Finally, I would like to thank Larry Kugler, the Acting Provost, for his support and encouragement; Donna Ullrich, the Director of University Relations and Julie Doty on the Ann Arbor Campus for their assistance in preparing the manuscript for publication; Stan Blood and Paul Gifford for photographs; Michael Ashby for cover design and campus map; and, not the least, Dr. Charlie Nelms, the Chancellor, for seeing to the ultimate and practical necessity of providing funds for this publication.

> Robert W. Heywood
> Professor Emeritus of History
> The University of Michigan–Flint
> May 1996

". . . it is the faculty and the students together, in an environment supportive of learning, that centers and defines a campus community."

The Place — Flint, Michigan

A portrait of The University of Michigan–Flint must begin with a brief comment about the city and the region where it is situated. Flint has been and remains a city dominated by General Motors. Its people have experienced, sometimes very painfully, the vicissitudes of economic ups and downs, of prosperity and severe unemployment. But to leave the matter there would be a mistake. Flint more often than not is underestimated and its circumstances over-simplified, sometimes by its residents, frequently by those from elsewhere with only a superficial knowledge of the city. Flint and the surrounding areas, in fact, present a very complex tapestry.

Flint has experienced what many urban centers have experienced in the past quarter century: decline, transition, and metamorphosis. Populations in the city have declined while those in the suburbs and out-county areas have grown. Retail businesses have congregated in malls both east and west of the city. The city itself, the downtown in particular, has increasingly been defined in different ways. Education, a diverse cultural life, an expanding service economy, and a rich diversity of peoples have become part of that redefinition.

The University of Michigan–Flint, a commuter campus located on the Flint River adjoining the downtown area, has become an important part of the urban landscape of the City of Flint. While an urban institution, the University also has a broadly defined regional constituency of eight counties in southeastern Michigan: Genesee, Lapeer, Livingston, Oakland, Saginaw, Shiawassee, St. Clair, and Tuscola. Just as Flint has come to acquire meaning in a larger metropolitan context, so too has The University of Michigan–Flint come to acquire a wider regional significance.

A part of Michigan's system of higher education, The University of Michigan–Flint is located roughly equidistant from the mother campus in Ann Arbor, from Michigan State University in East Lansing, from Saginaw Valley State University in University Center, and from a number of schools to the southeast serving Wayne County and the Greater Detroit area. Flint itself, with a population of 138,000 and with a considerably larger population in Genesee County, is home to several institutions of higher education.

In addition to The University of Michigan's Flint campus, GMI Engineering and Management Institute, Mott Community College, and Baker College — along with several other schools offering programs in the Flint area — bring the number of students in higher education in the Flint area to nearly 25,000. Of that number nearly 6,500 are University of Michigan–Flint students enrolled in more than fifty-eight undergraduate programs and six master's degree programs. The downtown riverfront site encompasses more than forty-five acres, with additional adjoining properties soon to be acquired.

While Flint is almost invariably regarded as a General Motors town, and the automobile industry remains its principal economic activity, the city has become one of the state's most important centers for higher education. Flint is fast becoming a "college town."

Flint has also become an important center for cultural events by way of the Flint Symphony Orchestra, the Flint Institute of Arts, the Longway Planetarium, the Sloan Museum, the Flint Institute of Music, and a number of theater, dance, and music organizations. With its rapidly growing suburbs and out-county residential and retail shopping districts, the City of Flint is being redefined in a larger metropolitan and county context. The University of Michigan campus, city and county government facilities, banks, professional offices, six large churches, the local newspaper, and two hotels have come to define downtown as retail businesses have moved to shopping centers beyond the city limits. It is a downtown being redefined, and The University of Michigan–Flint is a large part of that redefinition.

From its early beginnings in the 1820s Flint acquired a reputation as an important regional cultural center. Touring companies, theater groups, musical organizations, libraries, and a community willingness to invest in education characterized this nineteenth century town, whose economy proceeded from farming, to lumber, to carriages, to the automobile.

The rapid expansion of the automobile industry after 1920, under the aegis of General Motors, brought both money and people to the Flint area. Flint and General Motors had become an equation no later than a decade after World War I. It was all about automobiles, and a city defined largely by that industry. As housing and other more immediate needs of a growing population were being met, attention increasingly turned to the need to expand the city's educational and cultural facilities.

The end of World War II saw all of those pressures and demands escalate, in part because of the influx of yet more workers into the Flint area, and in part because of the numbers of GIs returning from the war, many of them looking for opportunities to further their education. Education was a major priority for the leadership in Flint. Before long there was a convergence of thinking between that leadership and officials at The University of Michigan.

The Beginning

In the forty years since the very beginning in 1956, The University of Michigan in Flint has evolved from a Senior College, with a handful of faculty, a few hundred students, and no physical plant to call its own, to a regional university campus with over 650 faculty and staff, nearly 6,500 students, and an attractive Riverfront Campus. From a Senior College, with course offerings only for third and fourth year undergraduate students, to the four-year undergraduate Flint College, to a regional university campus offering a wide array of graduate and undergraduate programs — in the larger sense, those were the 'metamorphoses' of The University of Michigan in Flint. Only the most visionary in the early years might have anticipated the succession of people, opportunities, and developments that brought this all about. There were very few, if any, such visionaries in 1965. I suspect there were none in 1956.

One should note at the outset that the circumstances that led to the establishment of The University of Michigan's Flint College were quite different from those which led to the establishment of the sister branch campus in Dearborn, a development which occurred in 1958. In Flint there was a broad base of community support, the active engagement of a number of local community leaders (several prominent "movers and shakers"), and the initially instrumental role of the Flint Board of Education. In Dearborn, by contrast, the initiative and community involvement were nowhere near as broad or as immediate. The establishment of the Dearborn Campus was largely the result of efforts undertaken by the Ford Motor Company. General Motors — and Flint was and is clearly a General Motors town — had no comparable role in bringing The University of Michigan to Flint.

While the Flint Junior College, which is now Mott Community College, had been established as early as 1923, and General Motors Institute (GMI) the same year, there had been no four-year university in Flint, nor any university presence of any sort in the city until 1944. In that year, in response to a request from the Flint Board of Education, The University of Michigan established a Graduate Extension Office in Flint. This was to enable teachers and others in the area to pursue education beyond the baccalaureate degree and, for many, to take course work beyond their initial teacher certification without having to drive nearly sixty miles to Ann Arbor. The courses offered were staffed largely by faculty from Ann Arbor, though after 1956 numbers of graduate extension courses were taught, as a teaching overload, by Flint College faculty. The opportunity to teach such graduate courses allowed many of the Flint College faculty to develop and offer more specialized courses in their various fields.

Enrollment pressures in higher education across the country following World War II, a problem very evident in Michigan by 1946, led the President of The University of Michigan, Alexander Ruthven, to propose establishing "strategic centers" across the state as a way of responding to those pressures. Flint, with a population of over 160,000, was a likely candidate for one of those strategic centers.

Perhaps by no later than the late 1940s, Flint's influential and in some instances wealthy leadership had determined that The University of Michigan should establish a college in Flint. Flint was the only major urban area in the state without a college, and these leaders believed that the city should have the very best. They believed, too, that The University of Michigan's presence in the city should go beyond simply a Graduate Extension Office. The two most important leaders in this effort were Mike Gorman, editor of *The Flint Journal,* and Charles Stewart Mott, one of the founders of General Motors and a Flint philanthropist.

The College and Cultural Center

Michael Gorman had been the leading spirit in the creation of the expansive and ambitious College and Cultural Center, a development that eventually encompassed two libraries, two colleges, two museums, a planetarium, a field house and a swimming pool, in all some sixteen buildings at a cost close to $30 million. It had been a community effort, largely complete in time for the celebration of Flint's centennial.

The Flint Senior College was conceived by Flint's leadership as an integral part of the new College and Cultural Center. In the decision for a college of The University of Michigan as against an independent four-year institution of some other designation, it was understood that control of and all decisions regarding curriculum, staff selection, admission and degree requirements and the like would be entirely the concerns of the University and of the Flint College. There would be no local control over such matters. Decisions on all such matters, including governance, were to be carried out in accordance with the Regents' Bylaws and in conformance with the traditions and procedures of the University. In light of more recent suggestions that there be some measure of local control or, at the least, influence, over the institution, it is significant to recall the understanding under which the University first agreed to come to Flint.

Two proposals surfaced in 1952 regarding what kind of institution The University of Michigan should establish in Flint. While an internal university committee proposed a four year institution, it was the proposal of the Flint Board of Education for a two year senior college, which would complement the two year Flint Junior College program, that was accepted by the Board of Regents early in 1955. A short time later Governor G. Mennen Williams approved a $37,000 appropriation, which allowed planning for the Flint College to begin. It was perceived in the community as the crown jewel in Flint's College and Cultural Center.

The First Metamorphosis — The Four-Year Flint College

If institutions of higher learning, including the Flint College of The University of Michigan, can experience a confirmation, then 1965 was the year that it happened. That was the year the College moved toward becoming a four-year institution.

By the late 1950s, disappointing enrollment growth had led College officials to recognize the urgent necessity of expansion to a full four-year program. Before the Senior College opened, officials anticipated that there would be 300 in the first class, with an additional 300 expected for the following year. Within five or six years they expected that total enrollment would reach 1,000 students. Those numbers simply had not materialized. (Winter semester enrollments, 1957, 1958, and 1959 had increased only from 204, to 392, to 407.)

From another perspective, most faculty recognized the need to develop their own lower division courses, a strategy which both faculty and administration believed would facilitate increased upper division course enrollments. The enrollment problem was seen to be at least partially a programmatic one.

Enrollment and programmatic decisions, and the decision to embark upon a four-year program were, in hindsight, quickly made. The College's first metamorphosis was about to occur. For those dozen or so new faculty and staff, as well as the first freshman class, it was quickly evident that they had become a part of an academic community already defined. It was a homogeneous group in that they shared a sense of community as teacher-scholars; they shared an awareness of being a faculty of The University of Michigan, with a clear sense of what they were about.

This early faculty was a heterogeneous group in that they had come from different backgrounds, from different parts of the country, expressing differing philosophical and intellectual views — all of which, of course, led to lively, sometimes heated debate on curriculum development, policy priorities, and any other matter that might conceivably be seen as falling within the domain of faculty prerogative.

For all of that heterogeneity, by 1965 there was clearly in place a lively academic culture, a sense of collegial community, and a certain ethos about the place that quickly absorbed the newcomers.

Trouble with the State Board of Education

Ominous clouds shadowed all of the excitement of taking the first of two steps that, by 1966, would have in place a full four-year undergraduate program, and of giving added dimension to The University of Michigan presence in Flint. Specifically, the State Board of Education was raising questions about the expansion of the Flint College from a two-year to a four-year institution, about the appropriateness of "branch campuses" generally, and more broadly about the autonomy of The University of Michigan.

In the 1950s, several state universities had begun establishing "branches" in order to respond to anticipated enrollment pressures. By the early 1960s there was talk of a college in the Saginaw-Midland area, talk which apparently provoked a reaction in Lansing. Interestingly, it was the expansion of the Flint College to a four-year institution that became the focal point of collision between the University and the State Board of Education. Specifically, the State Board of Education made very clear its intention to exercise control over the expansion and direction of higher education in the State. General discussion of new branches and the more specific plans to expand Flint's Senior College to a full four-year institution, as a college of The University of Michigan, brought the issue to a head.

The crisis was to pass for a mixed number of reasons: the insistence of The University of Michigan on its constitutional autonomy in the face of Lansing and State Board of Education arguments to the contrary (at least on this issue); the strong views of Mr. Charles Stewart Mott (the principal benefactor of the Flint College); the determined support of the state legislators from this area — especially Garland Lane, Joe Conroy, and Bob Emerson; and the position of the Flint Board of Education (which had supported the College's expansion and which had committed itself to providing additional instructional space). Almost everyone regarded this time, with its threat of possible coerced spin-off from The University of Michigan, as the College's darkest hour. But it passed. In the outcome of this confrontation, The University of Michigan and the Flint College prevailed.

Growing Pains

The lesser clouds on the horizon in 1965 were not as threatening though nonetheless present. It was more than a bit evident that numbers of Flint Junior College faculty and administrators were upset with the decision to have the Flint College become a four-year institution. Some had anticipated the time when the two institutions might become one — an unrealistic expectation perhaps, but sufficient to explain some of the momentary antipathy and distancing between the two schools. Program development at the Flint College, as in Theatre Arts, deepened that antipathy, especially as the Junior College saw that it would more than likely bring to an end its own program at Bower Theater. In the long run, as the evolving missions of the two institutions more clearly defined the different and complementary roles for each, these initially divisive issues were of diminished importance.

Finally, as another kind of "growing pain," those who arrived to play a part in the first metamorphosis were dismayed by the constant community confusion of The University of Michigan Flint College with the Junior College. Michigan faculty who were trying to properly identify themselves were typically and simply met with the remark, "Oh, you're at the Junior College!" The problem of identity in the community and in the surrounding areas took many years to resolve. In some scattered neighborhoods it may not yet be resolved. More than likely this has been a source of amusement for the Junior College faculty.

The problem arose from the fact that for the first few years the Flint College shared space with the Junior College. Once a building was provided, the John C. and Isabella T. Mott Memorial Building, named for Charles Stewart Mott's parents, the situation was improved. Title to the building, however, was held by the Flint Board of Education; the building occupied a part of the Junior College campus; and it was difficult for many to distinguish an institution separate from the larger Junior College. Only one small sign, easily missed as one would drive by on East Court Street, identified the building as housing the Flint College. A shared library, completed in 1961, another generous gift from Mr. Mott, further muted a physically separate and identifiable institution. It was an annoyance, but almost everyone at the Flint College recognized that time and growth — graduates and steady program development — would eventually resolve these aggravations.

Even so, for those temperamentally inclined, it was easy to become a bit paranoid. Would the College be "spun off" from The University of Michigan, left somehow to survive on its own? Would the occasional difficulties in the relationship with the Junior College do some eventual damage? Would the Mott Foundation or the Flint Board of Education become too intrusive in attempts to define the future of the College? Would Ann Arbor sustain its interest in and support for the Flint College?

While these and other matters may have been occasionally worrisome, they hardly dominated the life of this still fledgling College community in the mid-1960s. In fact, there was an air of optimism.

Mr. Mott had committed an additional $2.4 million for the expansion of the very quickly crowded and overused Mott Memorial Building; thirteen additional faculty had been drawn in from around the country to join the 1956 "pioneers," and those additional few who had been hired in the intervening years; an expanded curriculum, including a set of rigorous general education and distribution requirements, was in place; and, not the least, a bright and eager freshman class of 170 was on board.

The freshman class represented a different generation of student. Most were recent high school graduates. The earlier students, appropriate to the Senior College, were older students — many of whom were returning to finish their educations after some intervening years, many with family responsibilities and jobs; and, of course, there were significant numbers of junior college graduates. This student mix prevailed among a growing commuter student population for many years.

It was quickly clear, for those whose Flint College experiences date from 1965, that they had become a part of a defined academic community — in spite of any confusion about that identity from the outside. It was clear to all that community had been defined by a rather extraordinary collection of people, including the initial faculty, David M. French, the Dean of the College from its inception, and its first students.

The "Pioneer" Generation

David French, Ph.D. in political science from Harvard, a Rhodes Scholar, academic administrator, and U.S. State Department staffer — advised by people drawn from the campus in Ann Arbor — had the initial task of recruiting a faculty. It was a remarkable assemblage of academics. To mention but a few: William Murchie in biology, Donald DeGraaf in physics, Harry Blecker in chemistry, Marion Ross and Virgil Bett in economics, John Lawrence and William Caldwell in mathematics, Joseph Firebaugh and Edward Calver in English, Dorothea Wyatt and Robert Schafer in history, Frank Richardson in foreign language, Alfred Raphelson in psychology, Basil Zimmer in sociology, Paul Bradley in political science, Alvin Loving and Glen Rasmussen in education, and Robert Cojeen in business administration.

The Beginnings . . . Mott Memorial Building, 1966

Paying Tuition and Fees — Flint College

Those first few years of faculty appointments were critically important determinants of the character and tone of the place. It was a group with high expectations of themselves and of the College. Together with the Dean, a small administrative staff, and an initial group of 167 students, a collegial community was founded in 1956 and was securely in place by 1965.

While from varied backgrounds and different parts of the country, the initial faculty had proceeded from certain assumptions about being a College of The University of Michigan. There was first of all the mandate set forth in what had been the blueprint for the College: *The Dorr Committee Report* of 1955, sometimes referred to as the *Gray Book*. That report, in fact, cast a long and constructive shadow over the following four decades. The committee included senior Ann Arbor professorial and administrative staff and was chaired by Harold Dorr, Dean of Statewide Education. Working with Dean French, it spelled out the initial curriculum for the Senior College in anticipation of the arrival of the faculty and the first students. The *Gray Book* was the academic program blueprint for the Flint Senior College.

The *Dorr Report* . . . The first of the Founding Documents

The *Dorr Report* was explicit on a range of matters, which have had continuing consequence for the campus community. For example, the report stated that the College would be established as "a self-governing educational unit with the position, authority, and institutional relationships established for the colleges and schools of the Ann Arbor campus." The professorial staff were to be "the governing faculty" of the College with responsibilities for establishing courses of instruction, requirements for admission and graduation, and related concerns of the College "except to the extent that such affairs are placed in charge of the Dean."

The traditions and forms of faculty governance and of shared governance, which have been the source of occasional contention and confrontation between faculty and administration, have roots going back to the very early days of the Flint College. Indeed, they derive from The University of Michigan itself. They were not created by the Dorr Committee, nor were they the result of clever machinations by the Flint College faculty. Those traditions and forms were conveyed to those who arrived in 1965, when they were informed that the Flint College, with its specially designed flag, was in fact the seventeenth college of The University of Michigan and therefore, with its faculty, an integral part of that system. One added and very good reason for the strong commitment to University of Michigan traditions and values was the fact that eight of the seventeen full-time faculty with doctorates as of 1959 were University of Michigan doctorates.

There was more that, by 1965, had been defined and established. A great deal of it, in fact, derived from the *Dorr Report*. The curricula and academic programs were centered on a firm foundation in the liberal arts and sciences. A liberal arts focus, which included the significant numbers of students in elementary and secondary education teacher certificate programs, and in business administration, was secured at an early stage. The issue was a heated one, as some argued that liberal arts requirements left too little time for needed courses in the professional areas. Nonetheless, the values and traditions of a liberal education were identified as the very core of the College's mission.

Initially, the only degree offered was the bachelor of arts, so standard baccalaureate degree requirements were established for everyone. While this was to change with the establishment of new degree programs and additional instructional units at the Flint campus, there have been significant consequences of this initial circumstance.

The liberal arts and sciences remained the central focus in successive campus mission statements, although that centrality was to become a major question mark by the mid-1990s. The College of Arts and Sciences, nonetheless, has retained principal instructional responsibility for general education and distribution requirements in an evolving partnership with the several professional schools and programs established in later years.

Interestingly, the Education faculty have so far (1996) chosen to remain a department within the College of Arts and Sciences, in part underscoring the long and close working association with the faculty in the social sciences, natural sciences, and the humanities. This is an unusual pattern in higher education, and another element in that long shadow cast by the *Dorr Report*.

In some areas the shadow did not prove so enduring. *The Dorr Report* anticipated a staff that would be expected to live in the Flint area — a "resident faculty" — thereby perhaps helping give early form, presence and dimension to the College. Generally, faculty and staff over the first twenty years did live in Flint or one of its nearby suburbs. That, of course, had never been an explicit requirement though perhaps it had been conveyed to newcomers as a general expectation.

In the last twenty years, ever-growing numbers of faculty and staff have chosen to live some considerable distance from the Flint campus. This has had identifiable consequences for teaching schedules, faculty availability, and the campus culture. While some faculty living considerable distances from campus are on campus four and five days a week, many others have sought and obtained two or three day a week schedules. In later years students increasingly complained that individual faculty they needed to talk to were all too frequently unavailable.

Many faculty, especially those who have been with the institution for many years, believe this development has had a major impact. The views of many were summed up in the following observation of one senior faculty member: The growing number of faculty who choose not to live in the Flint area ". . . sets the tone for students — they drive in, teach their classes, and then drive away." She went on to remark that while we talk about serving the community, that mission becomes very difficult when so many faculty ". . . choose not to raise their children here, not to vote here, not to shop here, not to attend any local cultural events, and not to develop any local and community ties." The result is that these same faculty, along with those administrators and staff who also choose to live elsewhere, have little opportunity or inclination to develop a real understanding of the Flint area.

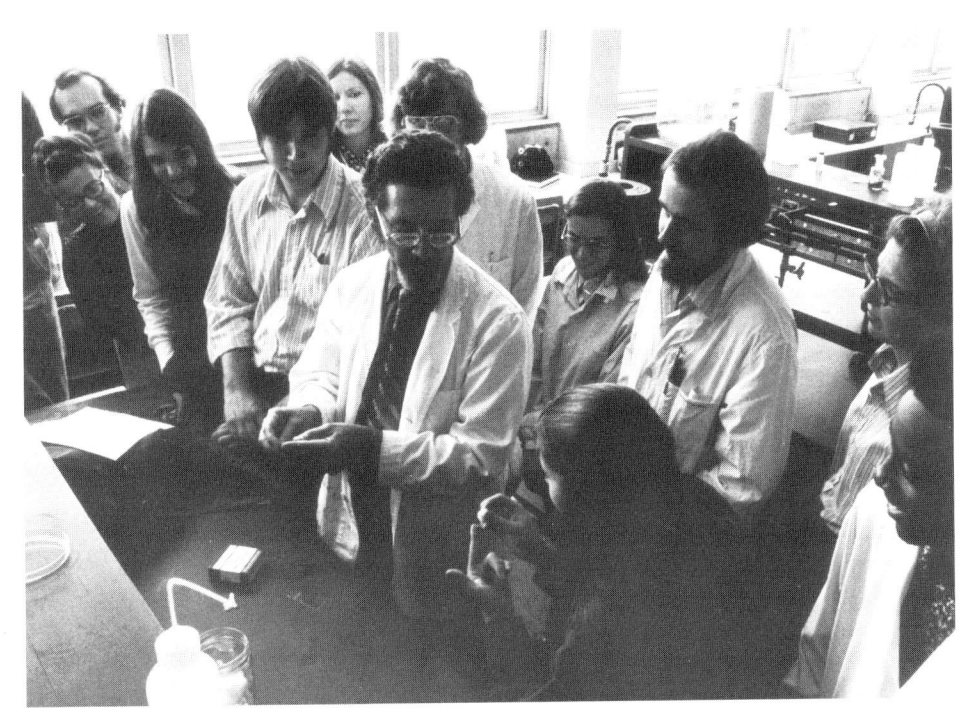

Professor Joe Otero — Biology Lab, MMB

Professor Bill Vasse — English Literature

Another (of many) unanticipated developments has been the ratio of full-time to part-time and contingency faculty. The Dorr Committee, and the early College community, had anticipated rather few part-timers. The Flint College was to have a full-time resident faculty. In 1956 there were only four part-time faculty. By the early 1990s part-time faculty were responsible for more than 40% of the instructional programs. Neither an increasingly non-resident faculty and staff nor a circumstance in which nearly half of the instruction was in the hands of a part-time faculty had been anticipated in 1956 with the founding of the Senior College, or in 1965-66 when the College became a four year institution.

The Flint Campus was not unique in either regard. Urban institutions of higher learning across the country have reflected similar trends with non-resident and part-time faculty. But this gets ahead of our story.

An initial group of rather remarkable people had created a College. It had its memories and stories; its achievements and its disappointments. There had been heated arguments and even angry voices raised at the always well attended faculty meetings. But most of all there was an overriding sense of collegiality and community. That early collegiality was perhaps foremost a function of circumstance. A small group of men and women had been charged with the task of building a College — with few resources, no physical space to call their own, no library, and little equipment. There was nothing of that "critical mass" from which one might just assume eventual success. But there was commitment and a strong sense of purpose.

Chemistry Professor Harry Blecker, one of the early pioneers, says of that initial faculty that they "had no doubt about their ability to build a College." He goes on to say that "Aside from getting our own courses underway, the first job was to get a set of bylaws. I was on that committee. We started out with the Ann Arbor LS&A (Literature , Science, and the Arts) Code and crossed out all that did not apply to us; then we rewrote the rest to fit our situation. Among other things this resulted in the formation of a lot of committees. Since many if not most of these required representation from all areas of the College . . . we got to see a lot of each other since most of us were in one or two person departments. There was a strong sense of collegiality when we were a Senior College and a relatively small faculty. Faculty meetings were spirited and well attended. Opinions were like belly buttons — everybody had one. There was a strong commitment to the College as well as our own departments." Professor Blecker remained for many years an active and visible member of the campus community, attested to in part by his sustained designation as "Mr. Code and Governance."

Harry Blecker also describes what must have been a fairly typical circumstance for that initial group of faculty. When he arrived at the Mott Memorial Building in September of 1957, the first year of full Senior College operation, he writes "the boxes of chemicals and supplies I had ordered had all arrived. They were all stacked neatly from floor to ceiling from the farthest ends of the chemistry space up to the door from the hall leading to that space. So when I arrived from Bucknell University, where I had been teaching, and opened that door, I was faced with a wall of brown cardboard boxes. I got Dave French (the Dean) to permit me to hire the six or seven students who had declared a chemistry major and we unpacked boxes, putting stuff in the hall until we worked back to the storeroom, then put stuff away properly. My students and I became well acquainted and the chemistry department went into operation on the first day of class. That is how it all started." It was a story with comparable renderings from one end of the College to the other. Improvising brought faculty, students and staff closer together.

The College Community — A Sense of Family

Faculty from those early years remember a sense of being part of a College family. There were the Christmas parties, with Dave French (the Dean) playing Santa Claus, with gifts for the children of faculty and staff. There was Virgil Bett (Economics), with his magic show. There were the annual picnics, which continued into the late 60s, with Al Raphelson (Psychology) as coach of the softball team. And there were the dinners at the French home where many a young faculty wife and her husband learned from Mary Ruth and David how to be a gracious hostess and host. There were also the Gilkey Creek Reviews, a sometimes raucous variety show of mixed talent and great effort, named in honor of the not very magnificent creek that runs just west of the Mott Memorial Building.

While there was a sense among the early faculty of collegiality, community, and even of family being lost with the transition from a Senior College to a full four-year College, for those new faculty who arrived in 1965 that was not the case. For the newcomers the Flint College was a coherent collegial community, in spite of the disruptive changes that some of the pioneer faculty found unsettling. Numbers had indeed doubled and eight new departments had been formally established. The Mott Memorial Building was about to experience the construction of added space, most notably laboratory space for the natural sciences. Trailers would soon be found in the area in front of the building as additional space became mandatory.

While sure signs of much awaited and needed growth, all of these developments distanced people. For a time (1966-67) faculty office space had to be secured on the third floor of the Mott Library, a library opened in 1961 and shared with the Junior College. Enrollments were such that rather soon classroom space had to be rented for a time from Woodside Church, which adjoins the Junior College campus. On occasion, classes were again taught in buildings belonging to the Junior College. So growth in numbers and in programs had their cost, in inconvenience, temporary arrangements, and a greater distance among those who until 1965 had been working in very close proximity to one another.

It was in many ways a matter of perception. For the newcomers there was a defined College culture, a real sense of academic community, and — fairly quickly — the occasion to get to know just about everyone. It was a time with its own excitement. If 1956-58 had been the formative years for the Senior College, 1965-67 were the formative years for the Flint College, the main difference being that in this second stage there was the confidence of building on the solid foundations secured in the first.

Where's the Library?

It might well be argued that no institution of higher learning, least of all one bearing the name of The University of Michigan, is worthy of that designation without having secured the establishment of an adequate library. This is a difficult and complicated story, some of which will be recounted later.

The College Library was at first housed in a corner room on the first floor of the Mott Memorial Building. Jacqueline Meeks had been hired in 1957 as Chief of Technical Services and Cataloger. After spending a few weeks in Ann Arbor finding out how the librarians there ordered and processed books, she then faced the task of giving some order to about a thousand books already on some shelves, some two thousand more in boxes, and more on the way. In the meantime James Pirie, who had planned the library at Youngstown College in Ohio, had been hired as Director of the new joint University of Michigan Flint College/Flint Junior College Library. The collection was to be a combined one.

In the process of starting the Flint College collection, there was a bit of entrepreneurialism. In the spring and summer of 1957, Professor Joseph Firebaugh, who taught English and American literature, had been sent to wander the book stores in New York. He had been given lists of books from his colleagues, but some of these books were not purchased and many books that were purchased were only on his list. Hence, some momentary distress: the purchase of some French and German translations, which upset Professor Richardson; the purchase of some metaphysical books, which upset Professor DeGraaf; duplications of works by Dickens, Hardy, Clemens — with no Chaucer, Beowulf, etc. — which upset Professor Calver. And so it went. Professor Richardson's distress, mainly with inappropriate nineteenth century translations, was sufficient cause for him to write in those books "Not to be used for Richardson's courses!"

As the story is told, more grievous was the fact that not one single book for business administration or education had been ordered, to the utter dismay of the faculty in those areas. Those book orders were only later brought to the library staff when found buried under Professor Firebaugh's other papers. As difficult for both the Dean and the library staff, no one had any clear idea how much had been spent. And, of course, one of the first and clearly very unpopular tasks for Jackie Meeks was to try to give some balance to the collection by ordering appropriate books for the education and business administration faculty. Fearing being tarred and feathered by the rest of the faculty (few faculty cared to confront Professor Firebaugh!), her problems multiplied when the College's business manager, Howard Cottrell, informed her that her budget had been overspent and that there was no money to cover orders that had already been processed. In the end some further $15,000 was found to handle the deficit.

A week off over the Christmas holidays, the hiring of Anni Hungerford as Cataloger, a new ordering system, a division of labor between Jim Pirie (the Junior College Library collection) and Jackie Meeks (the Flint College collection), some success at stealing book shelves from the faculty, the training of some staff — and the promise of a new library facility to serve both institutions — and things began to look better. Jackie Meeks' thoughts of resignation passed, and the Flint College had the beginnings (3000 books on the shelves by the end of the first year) of a library collection. By the way, for those who know her, Jackie Meeks was shortly to become Jackie Raphelson! Her husband, Al Raphelson, was the founder and long-time chair of the Psychology Department.

Several circumstances militated against the Flint College acquiring its own library building and its own separate collection in those early years. The agreement to merge the Flint Junior College Library with The University of Michigan–Flint College Library, and to build a single library facility to house both collections, was an obviously significant deterrent to the prospect of a separate facility, at least for as long as the Flint College was housed in the Mott Memorial Building and shared a campus with the Junior College.

The pressing needs for classroom, laboratory, office, and student space — for years — precluded much thought being given to a separate library. Moreover, there were always the libraries in Ann Arbor. While unwritten, it was clearly understood that library-dependent faculty pursuing their own research interests would have to arrange to spend some time in Ann Arbor when tending to matters of professional development. Numbers of faculty also assumed, from time to time, that research paper assignments given to upper division and graduate extension students might entail a trip or two to the libraries in Ann Arbor, if sufficient resource material was unavailable in Flint.

With the later move of the University's operations to the new Riverfront Campus adjoining downtown Flint, and with the temporary (lasting forever, it seemed) location of the library on the fifth floor of the new Classroom-Office Building, it became more and more an embarrassment that here was a campus of The University of Michigan without a "real" Library. It was not to be until 1994 that the Frances Willson Thompson Library was opened. But more on this later.

Jackie Meeks, Anni Hungerford — The College Library, 1957-58

General Education Requirements: The Bett Plan

We return again to 1965. While the Dorr Committee and early discussions with Dean French had largely determined the initial curriculum for the Flint Senior College, even before the arrival of the first faculty for classes in the Fall of 1956, it was altogether up to that faculty to work out an expanded four-year curriculum and deal with the task of defining general education/ distribution requirements for all students. The latter was the occasion for heated faculty discussion, beginning in 1962.

The mood was still pervasive, in 1965, at the College at least, that the charge of the Dorr Committee in 1955 and a largely sustained sense of academic mission still required a University of Michigan–Ann Arbor frame of mind and set of values. After all, wasn't this the seventeenth College of the University of Michigan, with its faculty holding professorial rank and tenure at the discretion of the Board of Regents of the University?

Curriculum, standards, concentration and degree requirements were to be clearly appropriate to a University of Michigan school, the only real difference being one of location. The Flint College constituted a "Far North Campus," nearly sixty miles north on U.S. 23, and the student population was a local and commuter one. The problem of how that largely traditional and liberal arts centered sense of role and mission was to be better adapted to an increasingly diverse student population and to the needs of the City of Flint, Genesee County, and the surrounding areas was only beginning to surface and then really not until the late 1960s.

While concentration and program course requirements were largely left to the appropriate faculty groups (really only a handful in each area), the general education requirements were the province of all — and everyone had an opinion. While the question of what general requirements would prevail for all took different twists and turns, the faculty ultimately settled on what came to be known as "The Bett Plan," or, according to Professor Virgil Bett, a variation of what he had initially proposed.

Having resolved the question of general distribution requirements (courses in freshman English, the natural and social sciences, the humanities), the question of whether to require foreign language was resolved by way of what some felt was only a political compromise.

In fact, there were almost as many versions of what the "real" issues were — principle? faculty politics? not very well muted fears and animosities that certain groups of faculty would benefit from one or another alternative? philosophical differences? — as there were people involved and around later to reconstruct their version of "The Great Debate."

According to Professor Bett, however, the reasoning went something like this. If foreign language was not to be specifically required, how then to assure that students have that or a comparable experience in a course sequence that would be both "basic" and "intensive"? He had some ideas, which he put before his colleagues. He then went off to Mexico on a sabbatical leave. When he returned a variation of his proposal had been adopted, though he was told "the Bett Plan has been approved!" The result was a Basic Intensive requirement, in which students would have the option of a course sequence in foreign language, mathematics, or in philosophy. That's how faculty work these things out — a mix of academic principle, faculty politics, and (usually) a reasonable compromise (though not often requiring that faculty be gone on a sabbatical leave).

In the long run, the Basic Intensive was to be abandoned and these initial distribution requirements modified as other instructional units, new circumstances, and additional degree programs were established at the Flint campus. In some sense, perhaps, the later "Area Options," though more expansive in purpose, followed in the tradition of that "Basic Intensive" requirement. And if foreign languages "lost" that initial battle by finding itself submerged as one of three options within the Basic Intensive rather than as a specific degree requirement for all Flint College students, it eventually won the "war," at least in the College of Arts and Sciences, by becoming a requirement for all B.A. candidates.

The Coffee Shop — MMB, 1966

Space Problems

With the new addition to the Mott Memorial Building, it was for the first time likely that the faculty in the several disciplines and areas would be grouped together in one place. More often than not that had not been true during the years of the Senior College. This probably had nothing to do with Charles Stewart Mott's frequently reiterated remark that he saw no need for faculty offices. (He may have had in mind faculty with desks in the front of class rooms!) It was for that reason that plans and drawings for the Mott Memorial Building, at least the ones Mr. Mott was likely to see, had only student and study areas indicated, and not the faculty offices which in fact they were intended to be. But faculty offices were secured, departments were defined, with chairs and — as circumstances permitted — with their own space.

Rather soon some departments found themselves ensconced in trailers arranged neatly in rows about the front lawn of the Mott Memorial Building. While these trailers were provided with reliable heating and air conditioning (comforts not always guaranteed for the residents of MMB as those systems were often down and, we all suspected, held together only with bubble gum and baling wire) — the trailers were without plumbing. Hurried trips in sleet, snow and rain — did the sun ever shine at such moments? — would find faculty awkwardly running from trailers to the building, for reasons apparent to anyone watching.

If this was an inconvenience to faculty and their secretaries, imagine the constraints and circumstances facing the newly appointed nurse/health counselor, Irene Roach, who was also assigned to a trailer. Her nursing colleagues elsewhere could not believe it when told that she was running a student health service in a facility with no plumbing, no running water, no sink! But the place was growing and there was always sufficient optimism to know that things would get better, conditions would improve.

The task of maintaining this growing facility was in the hands of, at first, Dave Beavers, and later — through the 1960s — Buddy Lyons and Bill Evans. They were essential fixtures in the place, doing and fixing everything, including the increasingly frustrating task of trying to keep the apparently fragile and temperamental heating/cooling system operating.

Living in the Flint Area

Flint College faculty, new to town and in a town unfamiliar with the work routines of a college faculty, found it necessary not only to continually identify themselves as a University of Michigan faculty — and not faculty at the Junior College — but to explain that "a nine hour teaching load, with summers off" did not mean a cushy job getting full-time pay for part-time work. In fact, as is true everywhere in higher education, many found it necessary to teach summers simply to make ends meet. How often was it necessary, though, to point out to neighbors and acquaintances that summers, a day during the week while teaching, and those otherwise apparently off-times were essential for developing new courses and for one's research — for that professional accomplishment necessary if one was to be retained, promoted, tenured and granted the needed annual merit salary increments!

These are problems of perception faculty everywhere face, though in Flint in those early years the problems were perhaps a bit more pronounced and irritating. Like good faculty at good schools everywhere, the Flint College faculty were held to high standards of performance in teaching, research and professional development, and service. In the years of the Flint Senior College, and of the Flint College after 1965, those standards were understood in the light of Ann Arbor based perceptions. That point requires special emphasis. The faculty at the Flint College regarded themselves as University of Michigan faculty who happened to be sixty miles north of Ann Arbor in Flint with clearly University of Michigan tasks to undertake. That self-image — one that proceeded from the circumstances of the founding of the Flint College and from the *Dorr Report* — absolutely defined the Flint faculty. Their actions and decisions in those years can only be understood in that light.

It is, of course, evident that growth in the late 1960s, a recognition that all of the University's functions in Flint (e.g., Graduate Extension) be administered centrally, and the need to be more broadly responsive to the area's needs and interests required some new approaches. While more was to come later, the Board of Regents' appointment in 1967 of a Citizens Advisory Committee that was to consult with the College's Dean constituted a significant first step. In one sense, faculty were to remain what they had been, and yet were to become something more by way of an increased sensitivity to and awareness of the community in which they lived.

The College's "First Metamorphosis" in 1965 brought about changes in the administration as well. While oversimplified, the management of the Senior College had been pretty much in the hands of David French, the Dean; of Robert Plummer, who had formerly been with the Junior College, as Assistant Dean; and of Howard Cottrell, as Business Manager. Within a short time (1966) Dean French was assisted by two newcomers: Robert Heywood, from the History Department, in Academic Affairs; and M. Joe Roberson, from the Flint School system, in Student Services. Joe Roberson, in fact, was no newcomer. He was in an early graduating class of the Flint Senior College. Joe was to have a long and distinguished career with the Flint campus, from Dean of Student Services, to Vice Chancellor, to Acting Chancellor, before eventually going on to Ann Arbor where he is now (1996) Athletic Director for The University of Michigan.

As Dean French continued to meet with the Executive Committee, setting College policy, the new Academic Dean organized a Council of Chairs, with whom he regularly met, and established an Institutional Planning Committee. The work of the latter led to the creation of a Theatre Department and gave initial thought to developing courses and programs in urban affairs, environmental studies, and

Black studies. Not everything, however, went as well as intended. Once, during a brief absence of Dean French, the academic dean — meeting with the College Executive Committee — had the group affirm the AAUP (American Association of University Professors) Statement on Academic Freedom and Tenure. The Dean returned, was slightly appalled by this administratively compromising action, and could only pretend it never happened. Most important, however, program expansion was begun and a momentum secured that was to continue in the late 1960s and into the 1970s with Heywood's successors in Academic Affairs — Bob Glenn, Jim Yankovich, and, for many years, Wes Rae.

There were other changes in administration as well. Dr. Robert Plummer, who had handled admissions and a range of student services matters for the Senior College, left to accept the presidency of a new junior college in southwestern Michigan. A sure sign of an institutional "coming of age" occurred with the appointment of Richard McElroy as Director of College Relations. With the College's "public relations" in the hands of a professional, clearly a new plateau in the history of the College had been attained.

Other new faces (Jim McGraw, Ken Bulmer, Ron Kopita, Annette Tenelshof — and, rather soon — Mogens Jensen, Ron Wisner, Dick Wise, and Chuck Rickard) were to assume the widening range of tasks, under Joe Roberson's direction, in Student Services. With increasing enrollments and more complex circumstances, tasks in Student Services had become more focused and specialized. No longer could one person perform multiple functions.

One of the most interesting developments in Student Services was the establishment of "The Head and Body Shop" — a designation proposed by the new Nurse/Health counselor. The unit was housed in one of the trailers and included Judy Smith, its director; Irene Roach, the nurse; Gary Rice, the placement officer; and Herb Crandell, student counsellor. In addition, there were student paraprofessionals. Mrs. Robben Fleming, when visiting the campus with her husband (then President of the University), was intrigued by the concept of a "Head and Body Shop" and impressed with the work of this unit on the Flint College campus. In later years, with a diminished profile, it became the Student Development Center.

Some of the key administrative changes occurred prior to the transition from the Senior College to the four-year Flint College. Howard Cottrell, the College's business manager, left for Ann Arbor. The word was that Cottrell had always tried to find the ways, and the dollars, to get things done. His successor, Bob Roush, perhaps in some measure reflecting the new circumstances of a changing institution, often was telling people — especially those new to the campus — why something couldn't be done. Some things could be done. By 1966 there was a new assistant business manager, Bill Borden. One assumed in those days that the College's business affairs were in good order when Borden was seen, inevitable cup of coffee in hand, standing about in the first floor hall of the Mott Memorial Building.

And then there was The Coffee Shop, second floor, north — before the completion of the addition to the Mott Memorial Building in 1967, which involved a less intimate and less interesting cafeteria, on the lower level, west. This early Coffee Shop was a great place for faculty, students and staff to mix, talk, relax, and relate. The Coffee Shop was where you got to know everybody. Much as building maintenance had its "institutions" in the persons of Buddy Lyons and Bill Evans, so too with the Coffee Shop. For some years Mrs. LeMay sold the coffee (for some, at half price if you only wanted half a cup). Mrs. LeMay from time to time noted those among her customers who were suffering from colds, and would add some of her "special medicine" (?) for a bit of symptomatic relief. She was no longer there by 1965. Those whose memories go back only to 1965 will remember Mrs. Johnson, a kindly, gracious, thoughtful, gray-haired and motherly lady whose very presence helped set the tone for The Coffee Shop — even though, on occasion and between classes, her presence notwithstanding, the room could get crowded and noisy.

The Coffee Shop — MMB

Flint College Students — Understanding Who They Really Were! A Faculty View

There was much that preoccupied the College in the late 1960s beyond developing the curriculum, worrying about crowded space and limited budgets, and (most fortunately) hiring new faculty. These were the years of the escalation of the Vietnam War, of campus protests — in many ways, of a heightened political and social awareness across the country. While it would be an exaggeration to say that the Flint College campus mirrored the tensions and strife that characterized many university campuses across the country, it is equally a mistake to suggest that Flint was immune to what the Sixties were about. Indeed, it has been suggested by some that Flint students, in the main, were too busy with their course of study, with their jobs, and with family and other community responsibilities, to take very much notice or express very much concern with what was going on in the world around them.

One faculty member remarked that there was a kind of passivity, a sense of it being a waste of time ". . . in making futile gestures; rather, it would be better to get on with the job at hand, at least for now . . . (and) this spirit of acceptance of things as they are, has been prevalent year after year, setting a kind of tone of resignation which rather typifies the student body as a whole." Reading that comment, one faculty member asked, "Were we really that boring?" The answer is "Probably not!" The truth is likely to be found somewhere in between, and more than likely not very close to that particular assessment. Much depended upon which groups of students, faculty and staff one thought typified the College as a whole. It depended upon one's associations and, even more, what one chose to see. By the late 1960s the students were obviously a variegated group, certainly much more so than ten years earlier.

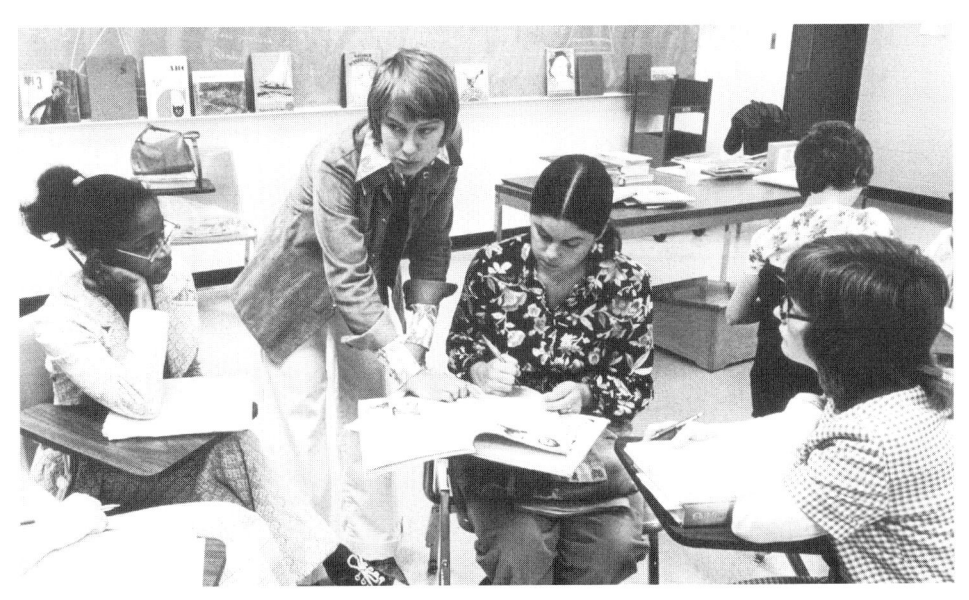

Professor Sue Woestehoff — Elementary Education Class

The Flint Senior College student, typically, was in fact very concerned with the task at hand — to do well with the course work and secure that University of Michigan degree. Careers were very much on their minds. Even so, there were clubs and organizations that indicated other interests in those early years: an active student government, a Film Club, a Business Club, an Education Club (since most students were in either Education or Business), some spirited student publications, and an Honor Society. Student life and interests after 1965 became more diverse and complicated.

For many college faculty and students, in Flint as elsewhere, the Sixties was a time when it simply was not possible for some, and not appropriate for others, to continue with "business as usual" — a singular focus on the pursuit of a course of study, a degree, and then a job and a career. For significant numbers, business as usual — securing the coveted college degree, careers, marriage and family — was hardly uppermost in their thinking. Social protest, civil rights, alternative life styles, marijuana, a shifting pop culture, the environment, the "new morality" — and much more — all came to preoccupy significant numbers in this post-Kennedy, Vietnam War era generation, even in Flint, Michigan.

A biology student from those years, now living in Atlanta, has a vivid and comprehensive recollection of those years. She says of the late 1960s, "It turned out to be four years of revolutionary change, for me, for college students on every campus, and for the nation. I watched friends walk down Court Street in protest of the bombing in Cambodia, joined friends on a bus to Wisconsin to campaign for Eugene McCarthy, learned on a biology field trip to Florida that Dr. King had been killed, and marched in protest with classmates at Atwood Stadium (Flint) where Governor Wallace was giving a campaign speech." She went on to point out that "There was a strong sense that even on the remote Flint campus, there were important changes taking place. Changes in how we related to our parents. Changes in how we related to authority. Politics came up at the dinner table. Most of us still lived with our parents. The draft hung over every male. Failure in class could mean the next semester in Vietnam." She went on to say that at the Flint College by 1968 ". . . most everyone was either a Hawk or a Dove. There were conversations in the coffee shop and the class room. A friend of one of the guys came back from Vietnam and sat in the coffee shop for a couple of weeks. I heard him talk about killing water buffalo. He had that weird kind of laugh and attitude that I have seen in movies about veterans and post trauma syndrome. Grooming declared your stand. Long hair and facial hair for Doves. I remember Dr. Caldwell (Mathematics, and retired Navy) explaining that his mustache was a recommendation from his doctor to avoid lip cancer and not a political statement."

While not as unsettling to the Flint College administration as events were to prove on other college campuses across the country — in fact the usual response was to make light of what did occur — there were numbers of students caught up in everything but "business as usual." On more than one occasion several hundred students (and faculty) gathered outside of the Mott Memorial Building to cheer anti-war speeches, one of them delivered by the then freshman congressman, later United States Senator, and early Flint College graduate, Don Riegle. Such events, in hindsight at least, occasionally had their comic side. Standing somewhat back from the crowd, in the nearby parking lot between parked cars, were several agents from the local FBI office — apparently to take note of who was there and what was being said.

On another occasion, in the spring of 1968, a student organization — the Public Affairs Club — asked their advisor, Professor Jack Schroeder, to invite anti-war activist Tom Hayden to speak at the Flint campus. After some weeks of frustrating effort, Hayden was found in Chicago, as he explained it to Professor Schoeder, "meeting with some friends and making some plans . . ." Hayden did come to the Flint College campus, where he spoke about opposition to the Vietnam War and the importance of student activism.

Not all students were tuned in to Hayden's message. One faculty member recalls the reaction of a business student from the back of the room to Hayden's remark that "Wherever I go on campuses across the land, I find students who are concerned with changing our country — students who are not just caught up in the money-grubbing rat race." The student raised his hand and asked, "You mean after I get out of school I'm NOT going to make more money?"

Many Flint College students never took the issues or the cause in anywhere near the way a committed SDS (Students for a Democratic Society) member, or a Weatherman, might. There were perhaps only a minority who were seriously enlisted in what someone called "the blue-ing of America." (The phrase, apparently, is about identifying with blue collar working people.) But the spectrum of commitment, and to some extent of involvement, was nonetheless there. It could be found on the Flint College campus, if one cared to look.

Marijuana was a part of that campus culture. There were then and are still now widely divergent views as to how widespread this was at the Flint College. It depends on whom you would ask. Some remember, for example, the smoke laden stairwell on the south end of MMB on numbers of Friday afternoons where one could get a high simply by climbing the stairs slowly and breathing deeply. Or the office Christmas party where some students had brought in a pan of "special" brownies, laced with grass, and placed it somewhat out of the way on the top of a file cabinet — the brownies only to be sampled by those in the know. To their surprise, and his, a faculty member (from another department) found them, innocently consumed quite a number, only to find himself unaccountably amused by anything and everything. He was later observed practically levitating en route back to his own office. There were always such anecdotes. But the incidence of drug use in those years is very difficult to assess. For many, there was very little awareness of such use; for others, it was a significant part of their Flint College experience.

There was campus reaction, too, to the assassinations of Martin Luther King, Jr., and of Robert Kennedy. Classes were cancelled on such occasions, as well as in the aftermath of the confrontation with the Ohio National Guard on the campus of Kent State University. There were teach-ins, where students and faculty would get information and exchange opinions on the pressing matter, or crisis, of the moment. For many, there was a deep sense of being involved, of being at a turning point in history.

There were, in fact, some very positive consequences to the social and political unrest in these years. Perhaps most important, the distance between faculty and students was in many ways diminished. There was more contact, more familiarity, both on and off campus than before. Especially for the younger faculty, there developed almost a sense of camaraderie with the students.

The faculty also proved responsive to student demands that there be student representatives on standing committees, those which enabled the governing faculty to govern. For some years this worked well. It ceased to work when, into the 1970s, the Student Government found it first difficult then nearly impossible to find the requisite numbers of students to sit on these committees. It may well be that students discovered that listening to the sometimes interminable arguments among faculty over some seemingly inconsequential matter was not how they wished to spend their time.

In another area, students came to insist on a curriculum, especially pertinent to the social sciences and the humanities, which they considered "relevant." Students' interests were considered not only in the development of new courses, but in the revision of existing ones. Courses, some of which were interdisciplinary, were devised which spoke to the expressed interests and needs of those students. While it is difficult to assess the long term effects of student protest and activism from the late Sixties and early Seventies, few would argue that the Flint College/University of Michigan–Flint remained unchanged and unaffected. The campus culture of any institution is shaped by its experiences and by the successive individuals and groups who set the tone on a campus. Flint has been no exception.

A contemporary (1995) illustration of a student body that could not justifiably be regarded as disengaged from current political issues can be seen in the decision of the Washington-based National Student Congress to hold its annual summer meeting on the Flint Campus. The University of Michigan–Flint was chosen over other contenders, such as the University of Wisconsin–Milwaukee, and the University of Indiana in Bloomington, because the rate of student activism was seen as double that of larger institutions. Student sponsored political forums and postcard and letter writing on a range of federal government policies — especially on financial aid programs — were examples cited of that kind of activism. (The USSA, the United States Student Association, representing student governments for 3.5 million students at 350 colleges and universities was founded in 1947 and is the principal advocate for those students in Washington.)

Nonetheless, one increasingly common feature of student activism is that, unlike the late 1960s and 1970s, students in the 1990s are apparently less likely to be mobilized by concerns over national and international issues. For example, affirmative action issues, student financial aid policies, and the long and drawn out crisis in Bosnia did not keep student attention for very long. Of far greater importance, apparently, are the concerns of special interests. The number and range of student organizations focused on ethnic, religious, career and comparably more narrowly defined agenda is a clear indication of the trend. The Flint Campus appears to be part of a national trend.

Flint's student body remains complex and diverse — a student body that defies simplistic characterization.

The Second Metamorphosis: From College to Regional University Campus

Within a short time of the completion of the transition from a senior College to a four-year College, it was evident that enrollment growth and space problems required that further thought be given to the future of The University of Michigan in Flint. In addition to the problem of growing numbers and crowded space, there was concern that the various interests and programs of the University in Flint be centrally administered and be defined by a singular presence. Any resolution of this matter would involve the Flint College, the Graduate Extension Center, and the MBA program offered in Flint by the Ann Arbor based School of Business Administration.

The task of addressing these and related issues and of charting a new and expanded course for The University of Michigan in Flint was given to an eight member planning study committee appointed by President Fleming in 1968. This was the Haber Committee, whose report in May of 1969 stands together with the *Dorr Committee Report* of 1955 as one of the two basic documents in the history of The University of Michigan in Flint. Within the framework of the Regents' Bylaws, together they constitute the founding and constitutional documents laying out the intentions and directions of The University of Michigan in Flint.

One of the most important elements in the decision to proceed with further planning was the decision by the University to acquire property and erect buildings in Flint — for the first time to establish a physical, real estate presence in the city. This decision was a radical departure from past policy. It implied a long term University of Michigan commitment nowhere near as evident in the earlier manner of a Senior College and Flint College presence in the city wherein facilities had been either owned by others, rented, leased, or borrowed. It was the *Haber Committee Report* which conveyed that expanded commitment and launched the second metamorphosis the campus was to experience.

The most important, overriding recommendation of the Haber Committee, in which President Fleming and the Board of Regents concurred, was that the University's Flint College should be transformed into a regional university campus of The University of Michigan. As Professor Al Raphelson, a committee member, has since observed, the president wanted a determination of the promise of the Flint campus, and asked the Haber Committee "to plot out a future for that promise." He went on to remark that this was seen at the time as "a great breakthrough for the campus, a campus that had received rather little enthusiastic support from anyone in Ann Arbor since the founding *Dorr Report.*"

Over the course of nine meetings in both Ann Arbor and in Flint, the Haber Committee recommended that the proposed regional campus "should be an integral part of The University of Michigan and should be developed with the expectation that the faculty and administration should strive to effect avenues of bilateral gain to the advantage of both campuses and communities."

At the first meeting of the committee, on September 4, 1968, President Fleming had emphasized that the University "is firmly established" in Flint, and that he wanted the committee to concern itself with a "long-term development plan" for the Flint campus. The committee thereupon identified eight topics that needed to be addressed: enrollment projections (to 1980); areas for program development in undergraduate instruction; number and type of degrees to be offered; organization and administration; graduate instruction; funding (operating and capital needs); the question of a chief administrative officer; and student housing.

It was a first-rate committee. William Haber, advisor to the University Executive Officers, served as chair. The committee membership included Judith Davis, a student; David French, Dean of the Flint College; George Hall, manager of Flint's Sears, Roebuck and a member of the Citizens Advisory Committee; Joseph Payne, Professor, School of Education, Ann Arbor; Alfred Raphelson, Professor and Chair, Psychology, Flint College; Everett Soop, Director of the University Extension Service; and Stephen Spurr, Dean of the Rackham School of Graduate Studies.

As a general point, the committee picked up on President Fleming's opening comment by stating that the future of the Flint Campus should be envisaged "as an integral part of The University of Michigan." Their report further stated that the University's development of the Flint campus should not be viewed simply as the sponsorship of a developing institution. Furthermore, a completely autonomous institution was envisaged only if, at some time in the future, "there is adequate demonstration by the University and the Flint Community of a mutual desire to end the relationship."

Until the early 1990s, during the administration of President James Duderstadt, this was never to surface as an issue — at least one which was given public expression. When the issue was raised in 1992, and some questions publicly asked, it became more than clear that neither The University of Michigan–Flint campus community, nor the City of Flint, nor the Board of Regents had any interest in ending or structurally altering the tri-partite relationship among the regional campus, The University of Michigan in Ann Arbor, and Flint and the surrounding areas served by the campus. Most continued to believe that there was great mutual advantage in a sustained and continuing relationship of the kind projected in the *Haber Report*.

In line with the charge given to it, the Haber Committee addressed the eight topics it had identified in rather broad and general terms. The task of a more detailed strategic plan was to preoccupy an Academic Planning Board in the years that followed, after the arrival of the campus' first chancellor.

Concerning the undergraduate curriculum, the report recommended that the Flint campus ". . . experiment in curriculum development and . . . be innovative in new ways to reach its goals unfettered by the ties of tradition, size of student body, and established vested interests of departments and programs." The idea that courses and programs should have interdisciplinary dimensions, sufficiently flexible to address new issues and problems, and that would engage faculty from varied departments and disciplines, all working together in innovative ways, was a high profile idea in higher education across the country at the time. Specifically, the Flint campus, because of its relatively small size, had to be concerned about the proliferation of small departments, each naturally anxious about its own turf, each naturally anxious to secure ever larger pieces of a never very big academic budget pie.

By the late 1960s, the Graduate Extension Office in Flint had about a thousand registrations each semester in graduate level courses, the larger number of them intended for area teachers seeking permanent certification or as part of a graduate degree program. The larger number of the faculty teaching these courses came up from Ann Arbor, while an increasing number were drawn from the Flint faculty. Flint faculty had to be approved for teaching these graduate courses by the appropriate department in Ann Arbor. The courses were Ann Arbor courses under the control of Ann Arbor departments, the University Extension Service (which had administrative authority), the Rackham School of Graduate Studies, the School of Education — in other words, an entirely Ann Arbor controlled graduate curriculum offered in Flint.

Two things were happening concurrently. The University was at the time significantly reducing its extension operations everywhere, and ways were being sought to turn over graduate instruction (as well as continuing education responsibilities) to the Flint campus. Toward this end, the Haber Committee recommended the appointment of a UM–Flint Graduate Committee, and a director of graduate studies. It was understood that graduate program development would not be in competition with or simply duplicate programs in Ann Arbor, and that such programs would be appropriate to the needs of the populations served by the Flint campus. The report went on to recommend that there be a "review" of existing arrangements regarding the MBA program offered in Flint by Ann Arbor. The assumption was that the interests of the Flint business administration faculty should be taken into consideration and that any resolution should occur within the larger framework of a single administration for the University's presence in Flint.

The issue of "one central Flint administration" was resolved by proposing that there be a single chief executive officer, either a chancellor or a provost, who would report "to the President and executive officers of the University." It was soon decided that the individual was to be a chancellor, reporting to the president.

As the chief academic official, on certain matters he would work with the Vice President for Academic Affairs.

Regarding student housing, the report suggested that the University consider "potential private developers" for such housing, and that once this approach had been fully utilized, then consideration might be given to University owned housing. In fact, one such experiment, the use of two apartment buildings on Longway Boulevard, was tried. The results were less than satisfactory. Distance from the campus, location, declining student interest in those facilities, and a variety of other concerns led the campus to abandon this experiment. This unsuccessful experience precluded much consideration being given to other possibilities for some years. There were a number of faculty, nevertheless, who continued to press the matter — most notably mathematics Professor William Caldwell and foreign languages Professor Frank Richardson. Both believed that the addition of a resident student population to the larger numbers of commuter students was essential to the intellectual and cultural health of the campus community. Increasing numbers of faculty, and some of the administrative staff, came to share that view.

Undoubtedly a factor in any discussion of possible student housing was the view of Charles Stewart Mott, the principal benefactor of the campus, that dormitories would be inappropriate for a campus intended to serve the bright young men and women of the Flint area unable for a variety of reasons to go away to school. Dormitories, or other forms of student housing, simply were not part of his thinking about the campus. Neither did that kind of thinking, to any significant degree at least, find expression in the Flint community. More immediately, other facilities' needs were regarded as more pressing and hence received more priority. It has only been in recent years that serious thought has once again been given to the issue of student housing. And even now, in the mid-1990s, other programmatic concerns are given higher priority and getting more attention. Student housing advocates still find themselves on the periphery.

Finally, the *Haber Report* recommended against a separate state appropriation for the Flint campus. The committee believed that if Flint's budget appropriation remained a part of the University's general appropriation, then the Ann Arbor administration would remain aware and sensitive to Flint's needs. In fact, it didn't turn out this way. Flint was to have a separate appropriation — largely the decision of the Legislature in 1970. How matters might have gone the other way is anyone's guess. Perhaps it is safe to assume that the President and the Regents have been sensitive, or not, to the financial needs of the Flint Campus depending upon who the responsible administrators have been at the time, Ann Arbor perceptions of the Flint Campus, the effectiveness of the Flint chancellor, and the general circumstances, economic and otherwise, of the moment.

Again, the central recommendation of the *Haber Report* was that the Flint College should become a regional university campus; that "it is and should continue to be more than just a facility for those who live in the Flint community and who might not otherwise have an opportunity for a university education . . ." and that "it should be an integral part of the University." In effect, this was a recommendation for both substantial expansion and for substantial autonomy within the framework of the University. Accordingly, as an operationally separate institution, the campus was for the first time visited in the spring of 1970 by an accreditation team of the North Central Association.

At about the time the Haber Committee concluded its work, the City of Flint and the Mott Foundation submitted a proposal for campus site development to the University. The Mott Foundation proposed to purchase a recently cleared site of some 17 acres about one-half mile west of the Mott Memorial Building on East Court Street. The idea was that the state would be asked to provide funding for a classroom-office building, the first of several anticipated buildings for this proposed site. These much needed facilities would complement those already available with the Mott Memorial Building. The Mott Library, a shared facility and collection with the Community College, would continue to serve the campus as in the past.

Toward this end the Michigan Legislature in the fall of 1969 appropriated monies to plan a classroom and office building, as well as a combined student activities and physical education/recreation facility. Architects had been working on plans for the classroom building for several months prior to the arrival of the new chancellor.

Chancellor Bill Moran

History Professor Dorothea Wyatt, Secretary to the Governing Faculty

Shifting Gears —
A Decade of Fulfillment . . . and Promise

The arrival of William E. Moran in July, 1971 to assume the responsibilities of Chancellor of the Flint Campus marked the onset of nearly a decade of historic accomplishment. He had come to Flint from the Stony Brook Campus of the State University of New York. Bill Moran was a person ideally suited to the task at hand. He was first and foremost a builder. His task was a major, even a monumental one: to lead in the transformation of a small college into a regional university campus with appropriate buildings, facilities, equipment, faculty, and staff befitting a campus of The University of Michigan. All of this was to be done in ways sensitive to the University's several constituencies, not the least of which were the City of Flint and the Mott Foundation. All of this was to be accomplished, too, in a decade of limited financial resources, both public and private. That so much was accomplished by the end of the decade is an enduring tribute to the vision, energy, determination, and varied talents of Chancellor Moran.

One of the immediate concerns of Bill Moran was that the seventeen-acre site on East Court Street, if pursued as the site for the proposed classroom/office building, would provide only a short-term solution to space problems. In a few more years further growth would lead to a re-run of crowded conditions, temporary facilities, and a need to secure a more appropriate site.

While recollections on the matter vary, in all likelihood it was George Hall (a member of both the Citizens Advisory Committee and the Haber Committee) who first suggested the 42 acres of urban renewal property located near downtown Flint, a site adjoining the Flint River, as an alternative to the East Court Street site. While some faculty and students expressed concern about locating the campus downtown, where they felt campus life would be less secure, the Chancellor moved quickly on the suggestion. Concurrence and support had to be secured from the President and the Regents in Ann Arbor, the City of Flint, the Mott Foundation, local donors, the U.S. Government, and the State of Michigan. The task of such a significant change of location was, of course, complicated by the fact that planning was well under way for the East Court Street site. Nonetheless the shift was successfully secured, a number of people were to later take credit for that fact, and in 1972 the Regents announced that the new site would indeed be the "Riverfront Campus."

Returning to the Flint Campus from his later responsibilities as Chancellor of the University of North Carolina–Greensboro in 1990 to give the commencement address, Bill Moran remarked that "the Mayor and City Manager and City Council members had pivotal roles to play at the outset, as did the late Harding Mott, and his father, as well as Bill White of the Mott Foundation." He went on to remark that "the city's business leaders were also immensely helpful, none more so than George Hall, and George Whyel." He noted that Dale Kildee, then a highly respected figure in the State Legislature — and later a Congressman — provided early and critical support for the Riverfront project. When all of this was in place, and when it was clear that the project had wide and enthusiastic community support, the President and the Regents added their endorsements. Moran was convinced then, and remained convinced, that the major reason for such widespread support was the hope that "better and more diverse academic programs than anyone before had imagined" might then be available at the Flint Campus.

While there continued to be those nervous about a "downtown site," others were soon alarmed at the way campus planning was proceeding with the proposed Riverfront Campus. Major responsibility for the initial campus plan was given to Sasaki, Dawson, DeMay Associates. SDDA was to work with University and City planners, within a broad framework of an academic mission statement, some specific goals, and a set of enrollment projections provided by a UM–F Academic Planning Board. Increasing responsibility for planning and site development was vested in a new office on campus led by Bob Wilson.

It was Wilson and, on occasion, the campus administration who were subject to criticism for proceeding with a plan that apparently envisaged no possibility of incorporating one or more of the existing structures on the Riverfront site in the long-range campus plan. It was quite clear later, for those who at the time didn't really know, that from the very beginning the working assumption in that campus plan was that all existing structures were to be razed.

While several buildings were identified by the "non-planners" as worthy of restoration and integration into a campus plan that would allow architectural and historical continuity between Flint's past and present, attention soon focused on one structure: the King's Daughters and Sons Home for the Aged at 517 East Kearsley Street. The principal and determined advocate for this building was Professor of Mathematics, Steven C. Althoen. His was a persistent and noble, if eventually unsuccessful, battle. The additional structures on the site, closer to the Flint River, included a number of houses, some of which had been the homes of Flint's founding families.

The King's Daughters and Sons Home, located on the southeast corner of the site, was designed by the firm of MacKenzie and Pratt. John Mackenzie, a Scottish immigrant, was an early and prominent Flint architect; Clarence Pratt was a civil engineer. As Professor Althoen described it, the style of the building was eclectic and concentrated on tudor and gothic elements. He observed that "the two foot thick masonry walls, the slate roof, and general craftmanship present a building that was meant to stay." Althoen also observed that "the time capsule in the cornerstone reflects a concern for history which does not appear to have been inherited by the present generation in Flint." With that comment, he probably had in mind the razing of the Palace Theater and of the old YWCA, both in downtown Flint, as well as the general predisposition to entirely clear sites designated for "urban renewal." Professor Althoen's efforts, in his words, to "show that the building is the best memorial to one of Flint's oldest surviving philanthropic organizations," to identify it "as the finest major Flint work of an early resident Flint architect" and to point to the fact that "it provides a direct link to the early history of Flint" were eventually to no avail.

The Beginnings . . . Riverfront Campus

The University acquired the King's Daughters property on November 1, 1977. For some time it provided temporary housing for campus administrators, as did the Brooks and Penfield apartment buildings just to the west of the King's Daughters building. Eventually, all of these structures were to be razed. Again, it is worth quoting Professor Althoen, who wrote at the time: "One matter of concern is that 'progress' appears to be systematically destroying the original village of Flint River — not only buildings, homes, gardens, and trees, but even the very streets themselves.... There are fewer than 40 residences in the area. A few of these, like the King's Daughters and Sons home appear worth saving on the historical ground that they are all that is left which represents an essentially unbroken chain of residency in the original village of Flint." It is probably safe to say that few in the community fully realized that the Riverfront Site for the new campus was, in fact, the site of the early Village of Flint.

Various faculty groups suggested a variety of uses for some of these buildings. Professor Richardson, the Director of the Honors Program, suggested that the King's Daughters and Sons building would be an ideal facility to house the Honors Program. A facility for visiting scholars, for exchange students, or — possibly — a faculty club (doomed almost as it was suggested!) were some of the other faculty proposals turned down as either impractical or too costly. Even the ultimate suggestion that it be used by the administration was turned down.

The building was razed in late September, 1981. While the University did heat the building, and performed some minimal maintenance during the brief period of occupancy, the structure was not otherwise maintained. The nearby construction of I-475 had caused some damage to the foundation, vandals had broken in and built campfires in the basement, and a leaky flat section of the roof had further deteriorated and caused some serious damage to several interior ceilings. Only fragments of the building were to survive. The mantel and a terra cotta plaque from the south peak found their way to the Hubbard Building, which houses UM–F Plant Services. The stained glass was removed and sold to Jim Fielder, a former employee of UM-Flint. Ace Tree Experts, which razed the building, acquired the time capsule from the cornerstone. This was later returned to the University, which then quite properly returned it to representatives of King's Daughters and Sons. Interestingly, one of the items in the recovered time capsule box was the first penny earned by the Bishop family, one of the early and prominent families in Flint.

The razing of the Brooks and Penfield apartment buildings in late 1982 completed the removal of all buildings that were on the site when it was acquired by the City of Flint for transferral to The University of Michigan–Flint. There remain those, perhaps only a few, who regret the lost opportunity to find some imaginative way of maintaining visible architectural links on the campus with Flint's past, indeed, with its early history. Viewing the campus today, whether from above as seen from the University Club in Genesee Tower, or from the City Lights Restaurant in the Metropolitan Building — or from street level — it is difficult to recall the campus area with its array of modern, brick, functionalist buildings as the site of the former Flint River Village and of so much of Flint's early history.

The Riverfront Campus

The first of those new Riverfront Campus buildings was the classroom-office building, substantially redesigned from what had been intended for the East Court Street site. Occupied in 1977, it has remained simply the Classroom Office Building, or CROB , efforts from time to time to give the building a name notwithstanding. On occasion, some faculty thought they might effect a surname change, abandoning the current name for "Crob," thereby after a fashion having a building named after oneself — or so the rueful comments went. Others tried to imagine an early, long-forgotten Flint pioneer by the name of Josiah Crob. There was even a committee charged with the task of recommending a name. The suggestions submitted were either unacceptable to the administration at the Flint Campus or to Ann Arbor. So "CROB" it has remained, and for some years it was to be the focal point of the Riverfront Campus. CROB was from the outset more than a building with classrooms and offices. CROB also had an attractive attached theatre, the result of the hard work and creative effort of the founder of the Theatre Department at the Flint Campus, Professor Gene Parola.

While the opening of CROB provided some relief from crowded conditions, it was still necessary for the sciences, including psychology and mathematics, to remain in the Mott Memorial Building for another eleven years, until 1988. During those years students were bused back and forth between the two sites, with classes differently scheduled to allow time for students to move between the two buildings and still be on time for their classes.

One consequence of the two-site campus was the development of a sort of bifurcated academic community, one the students were apparently more conscious of than were the faculty: an MMB science group, and a somewhat more diverse CROB group, which included people in the social sciences, the humanities, management, education, and the fine arts (music and theatre). For those eleven years the two groups constituted separate campus cultures. Some of the science students, who identified with MMB, on occasion were heard referring to their downtown counterparts as "crobbies."

The split was not altogether an even one, however, since 70% of the instruction was offered "downtown" and most faculty meetings, including those of committees, took place in CROB. The campus administration was also downtown, either in one or the other of the not-yet-razed buildings (mostly in the old Brooks or Penfield apartment buildings). In addition, some administrators and staff occupied rented space in the Ameritech Building in downtown Flint on Saginaw Street. These offices were later vacated in favor of space in Walker School just across I-475 from the campus, in the direction of the College and Cultural Center. A former elementary school, that property was for sale. One apparent advantage of the Walker School occupancy was that it provided a link east toward the College and Cultural Center, just as CROB had given the campus an anchor downtown. The Walker School property was not pursued as a possible direction and place for campus expansion as other priorities and needs took precedence.

Eleven years were to pass before a building was available for those academic departments remaining in the Mott Memorial Building. The new building, the

Murchie Science Building, completed in 1988, successfully acquired a name. The building was named after Professor William Murchie, a distinguished scientist, one of the pioneer faculty members, and founder of the Flint College/UM–Flint Biology Department. The Murchie Science Building is actually two joined buildings in one elongated structure, designed to accommodate the varied laboratory needs of the several sciences.

After 1988, and the move downtown of the sciences, the Mott Memorial Building was turned over to the Mott Community College (formerly the Flint Junior College). The University of Michigan–Flint continues to lease space in the MMB for the staff and facilities of WFUM-TV. It appears that Channel 28 will be the last to make the move to the Riverfront Campus.

While the move to the Riverfront Campus brought most of the University's operations downtown, a fragmented campus community remained. Not only were the WFUM–Channel 28 staff left at the end of the first floor of MMB, but several programs remained in what was at first called "The Surge Building," a one-story structure just south of East Court Street on Lapeer Street. More properly, the building, constructed in the 1970s as a short-term measure to alleviate immediate space problems, has become the "Lapeer Street Annex" (LSA).

While the "Annex" was for some years regarded as a temporary facility, it has proved to be one of the most durable of Flint campus properties. It continued for some years to house the Nursing Program and the Physical Therapy Program. The opening of the Murchie Science Building in 1988 allowed the Health Care Program space on the fourth floor; and the completion of the Frances Willson Thompson Library in 1994 allowed the Nursing Program to move to the fifth floor of CROB, which had served the Library as its "temporary facility" for seventeen years. The space was then remodeled for Nursing Program occupancy and for classroom purposes in 1995. This left Physical Therapy as the sole occupant of the Lapeer Street Annex. The effect, of course, was to leave the three principal programs of the School of Health Professions and Studies in three separate buildings.

CROB and the Theatre

Doubies — Downtown

Academic Planning for a Regional Campus

Building a campus, beginning with the much-needed construction of a classroom-office building, went hand-in-hand in the 1970s with academic program planning. The *Haber Report* in 1969 had laid down general principles and directions. An Academic Planning Board, appointed by Bill Moran shortly after his arrival and chaired by Professor William Vasse of the English Department, addressed the more specific detail of planning for both undergraduate and graduate program development.

The 1974 *APB Report,* the Vasse Committee Report, was both expansive and detailed. It was intended to serve as a blueprint for the next ten years. It projected a campus with a student enrollment of between 6500 and 8000 students, and it was the first campus-originated strategic plan. This document, which served as a general guide for the next dozen or so years, embraced many of the same premises and assumptions found in the *Dorr Report* (the *Gray Book*) of 1955 and in the *Haber Report* of 1969. It assumed the centrality of the liberal arts and sciences in the educational mission of The University of Michigan–Flint. Indeed, every mission statement, including the one drafted in 1985, has reaffirmed that fundamental principle, though the 1995 statement left it significantly muted. These later mission statements will be reviewed as we consider developments in more recent years.

The *APB Report* also emphasized the importance of the campus remaining an integral part of The University of Michigan system. The report further stated that the campus would be responsive to the City of Flint and the wider region it served by "emphasizing a basic educational core of the liberal arts and sciences, providing a number of professional and career programs at the undergraduate level, and offering a selected range of master's level programs that are related to specific occupational fields." The report represented an effort to give specific dimension to the rather broad goals contained in the *Haber Report* of five years earlier.

While it is inappropriate in a narrative of this sort to describe and discuss the detail of the Vasse Strategic Plan, a few observations are appropriate. While the *Haber Report* had warned against over-specialization and the incremental addition of small departments and, instead, urged interdisciplinary and multidisciplinary approaches, the Vasse Report reaffirmed department-based programs and then added that multidisciplinary programs might be appropriate in certain areas such as ethnic and area studies, and urban and environmental studies. The emphasis had shifted. Perhaps realistically the Vasse Committee had concluded that departments had become so fully entrenched that any alternative of grouping faculty and courses would be doomed to failure. There was some brief discussion of organizing divisions (humanities, social sciences, etc.) comparable to what had been done at the Dearborn Campus, but those suggestions found little support among the faculty.

What was clear by the mid-1970s, and what remains clear to this day, is that the faculty who have been drawn to the Flint Campus have more often than not been a traditionally defined, discipline-based faculty. While there have been some very successful interdisciplinary and multidisciplinary programs, there never have been very many and they certainly have not been centrally characteristic of academic programs at The University of Michigan–Flint.

The *APB Report* anticipated that multidisciplinary approaches might be most appropriate in graduate program development. The later Master's in Liberal Studies (MLS) in American Culture and the Master's in Public Administration (MPA) are good examples of that idea finding eventual implementation.

Some undergraduate programs and courses might be mentioned as examples of what has been done in interdisciplinary programming. Among the earliest were programs in Urban Studies and African American Studies. Both had been established in the late 1960s. Later programs in environmental studies, a minor in international studies, a minor in women's and gender studies, a minor in law and society, and the lower division work in the Honors Program are illustrations of successful efforts in this direction. Finally, a number of individual courses, many of them team taught, indicate an interest by faculty and students in courses that reach beyond traditional disciplines.

Among its fifty specific recommendations, the *APB Report* identified a number of undergraduate program areas requiring further development and new resources. Anthropology, computer sciences, geography, the fine arts (music, graphic arts, dance), and communication were specifically mentioned. In the more than two decades since, progress has been uneven in these areas. The reasons are the usual ones: limited resources, other priorities identified in later years, and — not the least — the fact that academic programs (the instructional programs) were found to have a declining share of the campus operating budget over those next twenty years.

The heart of the 1974 APB's fifty recommendations pointed toward program development in five principal areas. Attention and funding were to be devoted to 1) developing a program in the fine and applied arts; 2) further development of professional and career-oriented programs; 3) creating new programs in these areas; 4) encouraging multidisciplinary program design; and 5) finding new ways to respond to the metropolitan region and larger service area. Some of this was accomplished; some was not.

While this is not the place to examine the detail of a strategic planning document, it is the place to try to understand what such documents can tell us about the campus culture, its perspectives and values, at a given point in time. Looking at the mid-1970s in this manner, a sense of how that academic community regarded itself becomes clear. There was, first of all, great excitement at the prospects of "a real campus," new buildings, a fresh start, growth, and the prospect of being able to do new things. The Flint College was history; The University of Michigan–Flint was now the new threshold.

There were major developments in the 1970s, even as academic and campus planning proceeded. In 1974 the Bachelor of Science in Nursing was offered in Flint, in conjunction with the School of Nursing in Ann Arbor. In 1975, the School of Management was established. Until that time the business faculty had remained a department within the one instructional unit, with its essentially arts and sciences faculty, and with its roots in the initial Flint College. The University of Michigan–Flint had become a multiple school campus, offering an array of degree programs.

In 1977 not only did the Classroom Office Building open and the move to the Riverfront Campus begin, but also that same year the Master's in Liberal Studies in American Culture, a Rackham Graduate School approved program, was established. In 1978, the position of Provost and Vice Chancellor for Academic Affairs was established. The decade's conclusion was marked by the departure of Bill Moran, who had accepted an appointment as Chancellor of The University of North Carolina–Greensboro, and by the opening of the Harding Mott University Center. There had been momentous accomplishment and change during the tenure of Bill Moran. Some further developments were the result of faculty initiatives. The Honors Program stands as a good example.

The Honors Program

A much needed development occurred in the late 1970s with the establishment of an Honors Program. Initially housed in the College of Arts and Sciences, it later drew students from the School of Management and the Physical Therapy Program. When that happened it became a University Honors Program. In retrospect, it seems odd that it was more than twenty years before someone came up with a specific proposal for such a program.

The Honors Program idea surfaced following a College of Arts and Sciences faculty meeting in the Fall of 1977 at which much of the discussion concerned what to do for students requiring remedial work — for those students who were "academically challenged." A timely and fortuitous meeting of Professors Richardson (Foreign Languages) and Caldwell (Mathematics) in the men's room following that meeting gave rise to the observation that "no one seemed concerned about the needs of really bright students being tossed willy-nilly into the waters of mediocrity that will surround them for four years at Athens-on-Flint." This is the recollection of Professor Richardson, who went on to say that "the evident preoccupation with the needs of 'disadvantaged' students, especially, it seemed, by social science faculty, demanded that someone in CAS address the very real needs of bright students." That is what a few faculty set out to do.

A committee of eight faculty, chaired by Professor Richardson, was soon formed. The working premise was two-fold: first, that bright students, contrary to the conventional wisdom, needed and should be given special attention; and, second, that these students needed to be intellectually challenged. As the first Director of the Honors Program was later to remark: "We get these bright kids who have spent their last four years as big frogs in very small ponds, who have never been pushed to find out their real limits, never seriously challenged, and who, as a result, possess little more than slumbering potential." The Honors Program was designed to meet the needs of these students.

Most faculty agreed that an Honors Program was essential if the campus (and the College of Arts and Sciences in particular) was going to continue to attract and retain academically superior students. There was already some indication by the late 1970s that very bright students were interested in transferring elsewhere. It was expected, too, that an Honors Program would attract exceptional students to the Flint Campus who might have otherwise gone elsewhere.

The Honors Program was to have two primary dimensions: first, a "tightly structured, demanding core experience" and, second, an opportunity for the honors students to give "full expression to their own initiative, inventiveness and imagination in individually designed directed study and independent research projects, both on and off the campus." The distinctive features of this program balanced "Great Books," "Great Ideas," and an interdisciplinary senior seminar on the one side with disciplinary defined directed readings, off-campus study, and a senior honors thesis on the other.

Chancellor Moran soon provided the funding necessary for the Honors Program to get underway in the fall of 1979 with its first group of 17 students. Bill Vasse, the Acting Chancellor who followed Moran, provided additional funding for enrichment activities: the annual trip to Stratford, Ontario, trips to Toronto, and museum trips. The first off-campus student research projects were in 1982. Since then (to 1995) 117 honors students have pursued their senior thesis projects elsewhere in the United States and in 24 foreign countries.

Frank Richardson served as Director of the Honors Program from 1979 to 1991. In every important sense the idea, the initiative, the persistence, the conceptual framework, and the structure of the program were his. Under his direction it developed first as a successful program in CAS and then evolved into a University Honors Program. Eventually there were five programs available: a Freshman/Sophomore College Honors Program, a Junior/Senior Honors Concentration Program, a CAS Honors Scholar Program, a program in the School of Management, and a program in Physical Therapy. Since 1991 Professor Douglas Miller (foreign languages) has been the program director. The director is assisted by an Honors Council made up of representatives from the several units.

While the Honors Program has enjoyed sustained success, it has not expanded with overall campus enrollments. The reason for this, apparently, is that faculty have been remiss in not encouraging "the best and the brightest" of their students to consider an Honors Program. Two other factors probably had a role in containing the growth of the program: the sustained institutional preoccupation with the needs of other student populations, and the consequent circumstance of limited resources for a program that provides tuition grants, support for off-campus study, and small classes. Programs like this one require a special commitment from both faculty and the administration if they are to flourish. That commitment has not always been strongly and clearly stated. Nevertheless, the Honors Program at the Flint Campus stands as a clear statement of high standards of academic achievement. It is not surprising that Honors students have gone on to truly distinguish themselves.

Other Changes

The 1970s, especially the years toward the end of that decade, years which for some blur into the 1980s, are remembered as years when there was still a sense of community, of one still being somehow actually consequential and of importance to what was going on and where the institution was going. What is clear is that in the 1990s there is more than a little nostalgia for the 1970s. Some of that nostalgia is trivial, some of it not.

Some remember the pinball machine, which had found its way from the trailer outside MMB to an unused office in the Sociology/Anthropology Department in CROB. When asked what it was for, the sober response from a member of that department was "It's for statistical studies!" Others remember the places in downtown Flint, like Hat's, or Doubies, or at Nino's east of town on Dort Highway — the last a favorite for some of the Vietnam vets — where students and faculty would congregate for beer and conversation late in the day; or, even further afield out on Center Road, at the Golden Coin, where faculty and some administrators took comfort in winding down the week and concluding (or at least discussing) what was wrong and right with the world. Not one of those places survived the 1980s: three were to disappear, and one was to experience a name and ownership change.

At one point, into the 1980s, Gregory St. L. O'Brien, who was then Provost, initiated a more formal and structured social gathering once a month at the University Club on the top floor of Genesee Towers. The food was great, the bar tab tolerable, but the more formal environment inhibited free-wheeling conversation, which is an obvious euphemism for the kind of venting and griping required by most faculty and junior staff concerned about their states of mental health. What probably ended this social experiment was the Provost's unwillingness to have his office foot the bill each time; the idea was that different units and departments would take their turn. As it turned out, very few were willing — or had the resources, for that matter.

The 5.09 Matter

One faculty issue that was cause for anxiety in the 1970s concerned those colleagues who had been on one or another kind of continuing appointment, generally as lecturers, faculty who had not yet completed the Ph.D. or terminal degree in their fields, and for whom the tenure clock or years of continuing appointment suggested that a tenure decision was required.

It was the view in Ann Arbor that tenure decisions be made for these eight or nine faculty. Eventually the Chancellor, Bill Moran, took up the faculty cause and agreed to press the case for these faculty in Ann Arbor, in effect assuring them continuing appointment by way of an exception under Article 5.09 of the Regents' Bylaws. It was a hard case and, in the eyes of some, may have cost the Chancellor some credibility in Ann Arbor. It was clear, however, that Bill Moran had agreed to take the hard road and argue the faculty case. He had the easier option of simply telling the Flint faculty that there was no appropriate alternative to a tenure review for those in question. There were two consequences from all of this: Some fine and talented people were retained on the Flint Campus; and, arguably, some tougher or more exacting criteria for tenure and promotion review were to be articulated a few years later. While there is no cause-and-effect sequence here, some newly phrased tenure and promotion criteria followed in a manner which suggests a connection.

In the years that followed there were to be no further "5.09 exceptions" for those with the tenure clock running, and the requirements were to become far more specific about the importance and number of external referees required for faculty tenure and promotion decisions.

Graduate Teaching Assistants and Contingency Faculty

On another matter, there was less meeting of minds. Instructional costs, numbers of full-time faculty, and increasing enrollments led the Chancellor to propose bringing significant numbers of graduate teaching assistants from the Ann Arbor campus to handle essentially sections of lower division courses. There was a predictably negative response from the faculty.

Bringing in large numbers of graduate teaching assistants seemed an inappropriate way to respond to enrollment pressures, especially as the Flint College, and by then The University of Michigan–Flint, had long prided itself on having students working with full-time professors, many of them with years of experience and scholarly accomplishment. What was not so clearly noted, by the faculty at least, was that some instruction had always been assigned to part-time, contingency, and adjunct people. Some of them, indeed, were at a graduate teaching assistant stage of their professional development; others were without the terminal degree or without much teaching experience. The irony, if it may be called that, is that the campus found it both convenient and necessary to increase the share of instruction handled by this heterogeneous group. Without question this group included some very fine and talented people. Rather soon, that is by the 1980s, well over one-third of the instruction was being handled by these part-time and contingency appointments. By the mid-1990s it appeared to many that it would not be very long before *half* of all instruction would be accounted for with part-time people. This was a continuing source of worry for many of the faculty.

In fact, the Flint Campus part-time and contingency teaching appointments simply mirrored a trend nationwide, especially at urban and commuter campuses.

One very serious problem was the compensation most of these people received. While administrators claimed that contingency appointment salaries were competitive, except in a few areas most were not and in any event were viewed by faculty as inappropriate compensation for individuals selected to teach University of Michigan courses. Administrators generally made inappropriate institutional comparisons to justify the compensation schedules they usually followed. These problems — the share of instruction taught by part-time people, and their compensation rates — remain serious issues to this day. Unfortunately, attention too often has had the singular focus on the aggregate mounting dollar figure for contingency instruction and the fact that necessary resources have not been clearly allocated in the budget. More basic issues, those of concern to the faculty, are often overlooked.

Numbers of faculty have observed that it is sad that the University, given the fact that its principal task is teaching students, became increasingly dependent on "contingency" faculty — a word that by definition means "dependent on chance or uncertain condition." Should teaching be hedged about with such chance and uncertainty? Shouldn't contingency, part-time instruction be scrupulously limited to certain courses and program areas where it is clearly appropriate? In circumstances of limited resources, why are there apparently fewer "contingency" appointments in staff and administrative areas, usually in the form of temporary support staff? Is this how a university should order its priorities?

At any rate, perhaps it can only be said that a principle was secured back in the 1970s with Chancellor Moran on the question of importing graduate teaching assistants from Ann Arbor. Faced with considerable faculty opposition, he set aside his proposal. In reality, however, the situation was assuming a life and a momentum of its own under the guise of expanding contingency instruction — as we have noted.

Shared Governance

In all of this, as in other matters, there had been traditions and procedures of "Faculty Governance," or, perhaps more inclusively, of "Shared Governance." The Regents' Bylaws are rather explicit about what falls within the province of the Governing Faculty. There is, nonetheless, some considerable ambiguity in certain areas of decision making, leading to what several faculty members have called a circumstance of "creative ambiguity" in which shared governance, involving both the faculty and the administration, comes into play.

The Faculty Code and the Faculty Bylaws, which are approved by the Board of Regents (first in 1962), spell out in some detail the rights and responsibilities of the Governing Faculty. The Faculty can exercise its rights and responsbilities as a whole, within its separate schools and colleges, and by means of its committees. Some committees are clearly decision-making bodies. Some are advisory. The executive committees of each unit, working with the deans, are charged by the Regents with matters such as faculty appointments, promotion and tenure decisions, budgets, discipline issues, and program development. The Provost and the Chancellor also play a role in these matters, but the central and defining role has clearly been that of a faculty committee working with a dean. Faculty committees have similar central and defining, i.e., decision-making, roles on curriculum matters, admission requirements, academic standards, and graduation requirements. Other faculty committees are clearly advisory, and usually the name indicates as much. The Chancellor's Advisory/Budget Priorities Committee and the Academic Affairs Advisory Committee, which meets with the Provost, are two such committees.

A recent development is indicative of the continuing difficulty in giving viable meaning to shared governance. In October 1995 Chancellor Nelms announced his decision to dismantle his Cabinet "in its present form" and organize a "Leadership Team" that would "focus on issues that cut across academic and administrative lines."

The new Leadership Team consisted of 18 administrators, one staff representative, and one faculty member. The Chancellor announced his intention to meet with this group every other week, and with his vice chancellors and executive assistant on alternate weeks. The latter group appeared to be simply a reorganized and slightly smaller Cabinet.

In the announcement the Chancellor pointed out that "Since leadership team members are frontline people charged with administering the academic programs and services that enable the University to achieve its mission, it is critical that they be fully involved in the decision making process." From an administrative point of view, some wondered what the consequences might be for the role and responsibilities of the Provost. If the Chancellor would be meeting with the Dean and Directors bi-weekly, thereby involving them "in the decision making process," how then would the role of the Provost be redefined? What about the role of the Vice Chancellor for Student Services? Were the concerns of the Vice Chancellors only to be with "ongoing issues"?

It is important to note that, formerly, the faculty member (as Chair of the Faculty Council and of the Governing Faculty) met with the Chancellor and his Cabinet. This was a practice that went back to the early 1980s when Joe Roberson was Acting Chancellor. In that situation the faculty member, ideally at least, was involved in both the on-going operational and longer term planning concerns of the campus administration. This earlier and long-standing arrangement was a very important part of the system of shared governance.

The creation of the Leadership Team in the Fall of 1995 effectively removed the Governing Faculty from any role at the Cabinet level. It further placed the faculty representative in a large body (a total of 20) where it would be very difficult to adequately represent faculty views. The cost to the principle of shared governance was substantial. A significant role for the faculty, in this context at least, has been seriously compromised and diminished.

When shared governance has worked well on campus, administrators have been open with information, have been *serious* about involving faculty, staff, and students in the process *before* decisions are made, have sought advice and been open to persuasion, and have explained decisions when those decisions have been at variance with the views of one of the campus constituencies — faculty, staff, or students. Admittedly, this is the ideal world; a campus in which trust, communication, process, and community are all alive and well. And there have been those moments when it all did appear to come together and work the way, ideally, it might be thought it is all supposed to work. It works in an environment where the administration both trusts and values faculty involvement in decision making.

For all of the Regents' Bylaws, a Faculty Code and Faculty Bylaws, a Student Government Council, a Staff Council, and a Standard Practice Guide (for personnel matters), there is clearly no single campus perception of how governance and decision-making are to be understood and applied at any given time and with any given issue. It might be said, too, that the Flint community has rather little understanding of the traditions and procedures of faculty governance, if past *Flint Journal* news stories and editorial comment are any indication. That is perhaps not surprising in that the manner of an academic community, healthy and smoothly functioning or not, is by its nature more than a bit idiosyncratic, sometimes irascible, and — if it has succeeded in attracting the very best academic people — difficult to manage and lead. Small wonder, then, that there are varying perceptions, on occasion little understanding at all, of the nuances of campus governance!

Few, if any, contemporary institutions can make similarly seemingly contradictory and perplexing statements about themselves. From the vantage of simply faculty and administrators, what makes it all work is, on the one hand, an administration that proceeds from a recognition that the campus should be centrally focused on what faculty and students are about — which is learning. It is not a singular focus on the student, or on the faculty. It is on *both,* inasmuch as both are central to learning, scholarship, intellectual effort, and creativity. On the other hand, it works when faculty are aware of the larger context, the political and economic realities, and concern for wider constituencies with which administrators must cope and be responsive.

Staff interests, those of students, and — clearly — those of the wider communities served by the campus indeed make for a very complicated chemistry within which students' rights, faculty governance, staff concerns, and administrative concerns all require careful balancing if the academic community is to have coherence, some accepted priorities, a sense of what they are doing and where they are going. All campuses everywhere might similarly be described, in at least broad terms, even though particular circumstances will vary. What most would agree to is that while the chemistry of success is difficult and filled with ambiguity, by experience it is not mission impossible.

What makes occasional conflict likely at The University of Michigan–Flint is that both the administration and the faculty have been delegated real powers of decision by the University Board of Regents. They also are likely to bring different perspectives and values to bear on the same situation. What it so often has come down to, on the Flint Campus, is the attributes of the people involved — the skills, values, and talents of faculty and administrative leadership. When these attributes have been lacking — on either side — there have been difficulties. Sometimes the resulting collisions have been very difficult, even bruising, ones.

In some sense, trying to define "faculty governance," which is spelled out by the Regents and in the Faculty Code, is like trying to define "popular sovereignty," which is similarly spelled out in our Constitution and Bill of Rights. Both have broad areas of ambiguity which at best lead to a creative engagement of differing views and interests, *with a resolution which proceeds from a shared commitment to the central purposes of the academic community.* At worst, what follows is collision and confrontation. Little is resolved as a consequence, and, if decisions are taken, those decisions usually have negative consequences for morale and, sometimes, for the well-being of the institution. The Flint Campus has experienced both.

A Sense of Community

The growth of the campus in the 1970s and into the 1980s certainly made it more difficult to retain a sense of academic community, of shared goals and purposes. There were more people and those people were scattered, even with those steps taken that eventually would find almost everyone at the Riverfront Campus. More and more, as numbers increased and the tasks before the campus community multiplied, people went about their business increasingly distant and unaware of concerns and developments elsewhere on campus. This situation really stood in marked contrast to the earlier days of the Flint College, when nearly everyone knew nearly everyone else and when a sense of almost family had prevailed. Things were clearly different by the late 1970s.

For one thing, there were more administrators. The most important of these was the result of a decision in 1978 by Chancellor Moran to redefine his office. Until that year, the Chancellor had been chief executive officer with both internal and external responsibilities. With the creation of the Office of Provost, who was to be the senior Vice Chancellor, internal matters, which included coordinating fiscal and academic matters, and faculty and program development, became the concern of the Provost. The Chancellor could then concentrate his attention on relations with Ann Arbor, on legislative and other state government matters in Lansing, and on the wide array of community and regional interests and constituencies served by the campus.

New layers of administration occurred elsewhere. Just as faculty by the late 1970s looked along a chain of administrators, from department chairs, the deans and directors, and executive committees, to the Provost, and then to the Chancellor, so too in Student Services, where staff dealt with an array of assistant directors, directors, a dean, a Vice Chancellor for Student Affairs, and then to the Chancellor. These same circumstances prevailed in Plant Services and in other units across the campus where the increasing size and complexity of the institution seemed almost on its own to generate successive layers of administrative hierarchy. Into the 1980s, certainly, there was a sense of loss. And it may only have been looking back, as people will do, with a certain forgetful nostalgia that they remembered a lost sense of singular community, when indeed that singularity had never truly been there, except as one of those nearly tangible myths which helps give identity and meaning to a place.

However one might view these developments, it was the view of increasing numbers of faculty and staff that things had changed a great deal, and the changes were not in every way good. So the mood was a contradictory one. People were excited at the prospect of a real campus, the Riverfront Campus, and all that campus would bring. At the same time they felt a sense of loss and a sense of distancing, perhaps a fracturing of community; some experienced the beginnings of that feeling of after all only being a cog in a rather impersonal machine.

Not all of the restructuring was hierarchical, with new layers of administration. Some of it was horizontal, not vertical. In academic affairs, for example, the Business Administration Department was established as a separate School of Management, with its own committees and dean. In 1982 this new school was accredited by the American Assembly of Collegiate Schools of Business. After 1975, then, there were two schools: the School of Management and the College of Arts and Sciences. Then came a third unit, Nursing, and subsequently, the School of Health Sciences. In 1989 Nursing, Health Sciences, and Physical Therapy were brought together in a School of Health Professions and Studies.

By 1989 The University of Michigan–Flint, in academic affairs, was organized in three undergraduate units and the Office of Graduate Programs, the latter dating from 1978. Other units, as in Extension and Continuing Education, and in Cooperative Education, an Office of Research, and the Project for Urban and Regional Affairs (PURA) attest to the proliferation of units into the 1980s. The distancing and the increasing sense of anonymity was a function of growth in both horizontal and vertical directions. It may also have been the result of changing attitudes and priorities.

From the point of view of the faculty, certainly, those changes went beyond institutional organization. While it is difficult to date exactly, it was evident by the early 1980s that greater emphasis was being placed on refereed publications as evidence of scholarly accomplishment. This meant that an outside assessment of the significance and merit of one's work, by three or four outside referees, was required in all decisions for tenure and promotion. As a corollary to this, it became increasingly difficult to assess the accomplishments of those whose scholarly and professional development was essentially in areas of applied research. Examples of this could be found in the areas of local and regional research projects, some of which were being carried out under the aegis of PURA. It was apparently much easier, and certainly more conventional, simply to count an individual's publications, in areas of rather traditional discipline-based research, that had appeared in refereed and recognized professional journals. Some faculty were caught between pursuing traditional avenues of research on the one side and, on the other, following through on the institutional mission of the university as outlined in both the Haber and Vasse reports. Both reports had highlighted the application of the research and scholarly talents of the faculty in dealing with local and regional matters.

On the one hand, administrators in both Ann Arbor and on the Flint Campus were saying that it was altogether appropriate for the Flint faculty to define what "academic excellence," "professional accomplishment," and "significant scholarship" meant within the University of Michigan system, and for Flint in particular. On the other, it seemed to many that there was always some distance between the rhetoric and the reality. Traditional forms of scholarship and creative accomplishment seemed to many to be much more quickly recognized and rewarded.

There was something, however, more basic. While the reasons may be complex, certainly the increasing emphasis on publications effected a change in the campus culture in these years. The faculty as a whole became institutionally less involved, as evidenced by attendance at faculty meetings, the frustrating work of nominating committees in finding faculty willing to serve on standing committees, and the difficulty in securing quorums so that the faculty could conduct its business. This was especially evident in the College of Arts and Sciences, where a succession of deans resorted to providing coffee and cookies as bait to tempt otherwise reluctant faculty to attend. That did not always work. Faculty governance required participation and involvement; it required quorums. Matters were indeed handled, though perhaps not as expeditiously as in earlier years and certainly not in ways that reflected a broad base of faculty participation.

The difficulties facing faculty governance extended beyond any particular instructional unit, whether the College of Arts and Sciences, the School of Management, or the School of Health Professions and Studies. There were matters, from time to time, requiring the attention and action by the entire Governing Faculty. While sometimes difficult in earlier years, it was not impossible to secure a quorum so that motions might be made and votes taken. When this was no longer possible, a Faculty Assembly was established, in which each unit was given proportional representation. The Faculty Assembly, numbering some twenty-four or so, functioned as the legislative arm of the Governing Faculty. In time (the early 1990s), this was replaced by a yet smaller group: the Faculty Council. However else one might assess the health of faculty governance and the seriousness with which faculty regarded institutional responsibilities, the changing system of governance meant that fewer, in fact, were involved.

Other problems were to surface in these years as well. An administrative policy that was largely unknown in earlier years was that of granting faculty "reassigned time," or "released time." Administrators, unless they slipped into the more commonly used phrase, on occasion granted faculty "reassigned time" from a part of their teaching responsibility to handle a program development matter, a committee responsibility, or some other non-instructional task. Released or reassigned time was occasionally abused. The tasks involved did not always warrant a reduction in the teaching load. Some argue that these administrative arrangements were seldom justified. The obvious exceptions were teaching load reductions for those faculty who had assumed administrative responsibility for large and complex departments and programs. There was a time when a considerable number of non-instructional tasks were simply assumed to be a part of the broader responsibilities of the faculty. Yet some faculty came to see "released time" as a way of reducing their teaching load, as allowing more time for professional and scholarly development, or, at the least, as the only way they could be persuaded to take on some "extra" task. The problem has not been a major one. Only on occasion have faculty been led to comment about it. But the problem has existed since the early 1980s. Comprehensive and responsible guidelines for "released time" have yet to be formulated.

The academic environment was changing. Different pressures on faculty — including some seemingly new realities about tenure, promotion, and even merit salary increases — led many newer and numbers of the older faculty to shift their priorities. Those priorities were increasingly in the areas of publication, scholarship, and professional development. When they were met with pious declarations about the importance of "department, college, and university service," the response was often simply "Yeah! Sure!"

As many of the faculty became increasingly self-focused, as some phrased it — "busy cultivating their own gardens" — something of the character of the faculty changed. While that change is difficult to assess, it is likely that as recruiting new faculty occurred, a candidate's potential for eventual tenure in light of the new emphases was foremost in everyone's thinking. Some were to characterize this shift as from an earlier value on the "teacher-scholar" to the new one on the "research-scholar." The "teacher-scholar" was seen as a colleague whose first interests and talents are those of a teacher, and a person whose teaching rests on research, scholarship, and sustained development as a professional. The "research-scholar," as appropriate for the Flint Campus, was seen as an individual whose scholarly promise was given first consideration; an individual, as the expression went, for whom good teaching would be the "sine qua non" for continued appointment and eventual tenure.

The official and declared formulation varied from all of this. Officially and somberly declared tenure and promotion criteria clearly established a hierarchy of considerations: first and foremost, teaching; then research, publications, evidence of professional development; and third (though nonetheless important), institutional service. That was the official doctrine! Indeed, it did actually work that way sometimes. Though not very often. Faculty were quick to note the realities: Faculty whose teaching had received high praise, but whose sustained record of professional publication was found wanting, were predictably passed over for tenure or promotion; and the others, about whom reservations had been expressed regarding their teaching and work with students, but who were able to produce impressive publications, were almost always promoted and tenured. This divergence between formal criteria and rhetoric on appointments, tenure and promotion and the apparent realities faculty have to cope with is to be found on campuses across the country. The faculty hoped that the Flint Campus would somehow escape this circumstance. It's not impossible. Some schools, comparable in mission and circumstance to The University of Michigan–Flint, have managed a consistency proceeding from a high value placed on teaching excellence, on the faculty member as "teacher-scholar."

While the observation is undoubtedly prejudiced, since it comes from the Faculty, there nonetheless has been a remarkable continuity of very good teaching on the Flint Campus. Ever since the early years of the Flint Senior College, in the late 1950s, the faculty has taken considerable pride in the quality of instruction available to students. Where the continuity with the past is missing is in the availability of many of the faculty to students, an increasingly serious problem in the past 10 to 15 years. A number of factors had contributed to this by the early 1980s, but certainly the increased emphasis on publications and comparable kinds of professional development was a major factor. Another, certainly, was the fact that increasing numbers of faculty (as well as administrators and staff) were choosing to live some distance from Flint. For some faculty this meant that three and sometimes only two days a week would find them on campus and available to their students. In recent years, even those faculty living in the Flint area have fallen into the habit of spending less time on campus.

Professor Dennis Ellis — School of Management

While this is clearly the down-side from the point of view of students and in terms of the ideal of a close faculty-student relationship, it is nonetheless true that the quality of teaching on the Flint Campus has been very good. How do we know that? Mostly in subjective ways, though we do have an accumulation of student course and instructor evaluations, as well as peer evaluations. But much of the impression is gained in an altogether non-scientific, hearsay fashion: informal student comment, especially from transfer students able to make comparisons with their experiences elsewhere; and those intangible, cumulative reputations that individual faculty acquire over the years. For all of their other preoccupations, Flint faculty as a whole devote a great deal of thought, time, talent and energy to the task of teaching. From the Biology Department to the Theatre Department, from some unusually well-taught courses in the School of Management to the Physical Therapy program, the Flint Campus has good reason to celebrate the quality of teaching available to its students.

While there is evidence for continuity of good teaching on the Flint Campus, faculty perceptions of the quality of students has changed. Again, the Flint faculty found themselves with a great deal of company across the country by the late 1970s or early 1980s. It has, of course, become almost commonplace to bemoan the declining verbal and quantitative skills and general informational background that students bring to the college experience. Whatever assessment might objectively be made, in some comparative way with earlier generations of in-coming college students, it was nonetheless clear to faculty that students were less well prepared to deal with the range of course work facing them. Worries about lowering expectations, grade inflation, remedial work, tutorial assistance, the role of a Writing Lab, and — ultimately — how well educated in fact were the recipients of a baccalaureate degree from a campus of The University of Michigan were matters of increased concern, and even anxiety. Once again, this was not a circumstance unique to the Flint Campus. It was a source of concern almost everywhere in higher education across the country.

Professor Reinhard Thum — Foreign Language Lab

The Academic Community in Search of Itself: The 1980s

Many of the concerns and issues before the faculty in the late 1970s were to persist into the 1980s. The 1980s are a difficult decade to label — as one might, for example, have labeled the 1970s "the Moran Era," or "From College to Regional University," or, even more simply, "The Move Downtown." For one thing there was a succession of administrators, especially in the office of the Chancellor, but also in the offices of the Vice Chancellors and Deans. That meant some years of instability at the upper echelons and, to some extent, a resultant lack of a clear sense of institutional direction and leadership.

When Bill Moran left for the University of North Carolina at Greensboro, Professor William Vasse (who had chaired the Academic Planning Board a few years earlier) stepped in to serve as Acting Chancellor for a year. Dr. Conny Nelson, who came to the Flint Campus from North Dakota, then served until his early death in 1983. He was followed by Joe Roberson who served the next year as Acting Chancellor. Roberson had been a long-time Flint administrator, serving first as Dean of Student Services, then as Vice Chancellor for Student Affairs. He was to leave the Flint Campus in the mid-1980s for appointments in Ann Arbor, first in the Development Office, and then as Athletic Director.

These were not years of great accomplishment. One memorable academic accomplishment during the tenure of Conny Nelson, however, was the successful negotiation of the transfer of the Ann Arbor based Physical Therapy Program, with its faculty and director, to the Flint Campus.

On the other hand, this was also the time of an unforgettable and terrible event, the murder of Margaret Eby. Dr. Eby had been brought from the Dearborn Campus by Conny Nelson to serve as Provost and Vice Chancellor for Academic Affairs in the early 1980s. While her tenure was perhaps too brief for any significant accomplishment as Provost, many will remember her work with the "Basically Bach Festival." A musician, Dr. Eby also had an appointment in the Music Department. She was discovered to have been murdered at home. Her home was the Carriage House which she had rented and which was located at Applewood, the estate of Charles Stewart Mott and the residence of Mrs. Ruth Mott. The campus and community both were appalled by the news. To this day no one has been arrested and the murder remains an unsolved mystery. It was the event that marked the early 1980s. Most will remember what they were doing and where they were when they heard the news of what had happened.

Others recall the campus budget and personnel uncertainties that followed the severe down-turn in the Michigan economy in these years. The "fairly brutal staff cuts," as remembered by one senior staff member, left an enduring mark on the campus community. Morale was seriously damaged. While faculty were assured of their jobs, staff were left wondering who was to go and who was to remain. Many felt the financial problems facing the University at that time could have been handled more humanely and in ways less disruptive of people's lives.

The Jones Era

Dr. Clinton Jones, most recently from Georgia State, was appointed Chancellor in 1984, bringing to an end what might be seen as a five year interregnum. If not immediately in 1984, then following further cabinet level changes during the early years of Chancellor Jones' tenure, some newfound administrative stability was secured, certainly no later than 1987. Among those who left the Flint Campus in these years for appointments in Ann Arbor were Joe Roberson, Jim Murdoch, who had been Vice Chancellor for Administration, and Julie Cunningham, from the University Relations Office. Some, like Dick McElroy, who had been with the campus since Flint College days and who had for long years carried the burden of public relations and legislative relations left for employment elsewhere. Carol Surles, who followed Murdoch as Vice Chancellor of Administration, also left after just a few years.

Toward the end of the decade, however, things seemed to settle down with the administrative staff. The "Jones Era," a time quite different in many ways from earlier stages in the history of the institution, was in place. The long tenure of Larry Kugler as Dean of the College of Arts and Sciences, of Rich Fortner in the School of Management, and of Victor Wong as Provost and Vice Chancellor for Academic Affairs was evidence of that newfound administrative stability. The continuing presence of Dorothy Russell as Vice Chancellor for Administration, Joanne Sullenger in Development, David Palmer as Librarian (whose appointment went back to the Moran years), and Bill Webb in Human Resources gave further substance to that sense that things were settling down in the administration of the campus. As the number of administrative searches diminished faculty and staff could turn their attention to other matters.

Minority Issues: A Focus on Diversity

Possibly the single most important, talked about, and sometimes contentious issue during the years that Clinton Jones was Chancellor would fall under the heading of one or more of the following: minority initiatives, diversity, and affirmative action — a campus attempting to be more reflective of and responsive to the Flint area and its diverse populations. Perhaps an appropriate designation for the decade might involve those minority and diversity concerns that were ever-present on the campus agenda.

These issues were not altogether new. They were new perhaps only in the intensity and scope with which they were pursued and the priority they had acquired. For at least a decade prior to the arrival of Chancellor Jones, and in some real sense going back to the late 1960s, there had been a growing awareness that the campus needed to devote both planning effort and resources in ways that would allow the Flint College — and then The University of Michigan–Flint — to address minority concerns.

Until the late 1960s little conscious attention on the part of either faculty or staff had been given to such matters. Until then the idea had been that a University of Michigan education would be provided to all qualified and admissible students in the Flint area. It was believed that statement expressed all that needed to be said. In the early years thinking didn't really go very far beyond that premise.

When the senior college became a four year college, beginning in 1966, program development interests for the first time went beyond the usual concerns about general education and concentration requirements. The larger issues of how to attract minority students, what programs and courses should be developed, and how to reach a larger population became matters of concern both in academic affairs and in student services. While great and wonderful things were in no way accomplished, it would be a mistake to look upon those years as empty of concern and effort and barren of result. Rather early, certainly no later than the late 1960s, faculty in a number of departments in the social sciences and the humanities began to develop and offer new courses dealing with minorities. A specific effort to recruit minority faculty also had its real beginnings in those years. Earlier, there had been but one African-American among the faculty with a regular full-time appointment: Professor Alvin Loving, who taught courses in Education and who later accepted an appointment in Ann Arbor. These first steps marked an important beginning.

African-American Studies

Another major step was taken in 1969 with the establishment of the Challenge Program. The object of this program was to enable selected students, minority students in particular, who did not meet normal requirements to gain admission. The Challenge Program recognized that there were numbers of students who had failed to reach their potential in high school but who would likely succeed at college level work with the right mix of counseling and special assistance. In its early years this program brought numbers of minority students to the campus, students who otherwise very likely would have not attended. In later years the percentage of minorities in the program declined while the numbers of those from beyond Flint increased.

One considerable problem facing The University of Michigan–Flint in attracting minority students, especially African-American students, has always been a combination of tradition and perception. From the vantage of tradition, many of the best and the brightest of Flint's African-American high school graduates have wanted to go away to school, many of them to Michigan State University. That's where friends and older brothers and sisters had gone. Others looked elsewhere, some of them to schools out of state.

From the vantage of perception, there has been a persistent sense — especially in the early years — that The University of Michigan–Flint presented a less than friendly and encouraging environment for African-American and other minority students. This was a difficult problem in that it reflected sometimes subtle attitudes and behaviors on the part of students, faculty and staff, as well as perceptions of the physical environment of the campus. A great deal of time and thought has been devoted to a resolution of this problem, though not every step taken has been constructive. While much has been done to alter that perception, to some extent that old perception and the problems from which that perception arises, still persist. Changing an established image, whether founded in realities or not, is a very difficult task.

Professor Levi Nwachuku

Until the late 1960s the curriculum at the Flint College, like college curricula almost everywhere, was the traditional curriculum of higher education — experimental and innovative only insofar as some faculty had developed courses with an interdisciplinary focus, with rather little course content dealing with minorities. And there were rather few of those courses. There were almost no courses which focused specifically on women and minorities and there were only a few courses that included scattered material dealing with the experiences and interests of these groups.

Course development in the 1970s that centered on the experience of minorities, not surprisingly, occurred principally in the social sciences and the humanities. By the end of that decade there was a considerable array of such courses. One of the earliest was "The History of Women," developed and offered by Professor Dorothea Wyatt, the first Chair of the History Department and long-time Secretary to the Faculty. Some years after her retirement, the Dorothea Wyatt Award was established, in part in recognition of her advocacy of women's interests. The purpose of the award was to recognize outstanding contributions of women faculty and staff to the interests and concerns of women. Professor Nora Faires of the History Department was the first faculty recipient in 1989; Irene K. Roach, Nurse Clinician in the Student Health Service, was the first staff recipient the following year.

Many of the courses that were developed and offered during these years were cross-listed courses. Programs and courses in African-American Studies, in Women's Studies, and in Chicano Studies generally depended on departments and programs to offer and staff courses that could either be taken for department credit or, for example, African-American Studies course credit. Several problems surfaced. These programs became dependent on other departments as they had virtually no core faculty, or budget for that matter, of their own. Generally, departments were helpful and interested, but other course needs — for those with concentration requirements in the departments, for example — frequently took precedence.

It also became clear that very few students were interested in pursuing a concentration program in minority or women's studies. Most student interest in these programs, including that of women and minority students, was in a particular course or with a popular instructor. Only in the early 1990s did enrollments begin to suggest greater interest, especially in women's studies where increased numbers were electing a minor.

A related problem was the turnover of minority faculty. The History Department might serve as an illustration. For both African-American and Mexican-American history courses there had been consecutive appointments of minority faculty, all of whom eventually left for better pay, early promotion, lighter teaching loads and/or the opportunity to teach graduate courses. The History Department had nearly ten minority faculty over a period of nearly two decades, both part-time and full-time, most of whom stayed only a few years — all of whom left for better situations.

This presents a rather grim picture. In fact, there have been ways of seeing the glass half full, rather than half empty. There have been some very good faculty and some fine courses and seminars offered over the years, in a number of programs and departments, that warrant a more generous reading of the accomplishments of those years. The effort continues.

One decision of the faculty in more recent years was to include a specific course on diversity in the general education program. Dean Jacqueline Zeff was instrumental in encouraging this initiative. This course, developed by Professor Leslie Moch of the History Department, is multidisciplinary and has involved faculty from a number of disciplines. It was offered for the first time in 1994. While not a required course, it does represent a faculty effort to address minority and diversity issues within the framework of the general education program. The course has the title: "Made in America: Diversity and Inequality in the U.S."

An Administrative Response

The Chancellor placed high priority on a wide range of minority and diversity initiatives. In 1987, for example, Dr. Jones established an Office of Minority Affairs, giving Professor Benjamin Dennis (Anthropology) administrative responsibility. The office received a broad mandate: the development of programs appropriate for Black History Month, recruiting African-American students, the development of a mentor program, new scholarships, and other programs that would provide support and assistance for minority students.

By the late 1980s some confusion had surfaced regarding roles and responsibilities of a number of people and offices concerned about minority issues. Who was in charge of what? Beyond the Office of Minority Affairs, there were the faculty in the African-American Studies Program, staff in the Student Development Center, and others with special minorities responsibilities in affirmative action, financial aid, and student admissions. A strategic planning document in 1988 modestly suggested — perhaps as a bit of understatement — that "the existing dispersion of resources to support diversity and minority concerns might impede realization of our aspirations in this important area."

In time some of this confusion was sorted out. Some of it, however, has persisted. In August of 1995, for example, an executive director of Educational Opportunity Initiatives was appointed. That position had formerly been the executive assistant to the chancellor for Multicultural Initiatives. The new position involved coordinating all efforts designed to enhance minority student enrollment and retention. But what had become of the other task: multicultural initiatives? What, exactly, was being coordinated? Undoubtedly, there were those who knew. But there were many who did not.

Problems Emerge

Especially during the late 1980s and into the early 1990s, many of the faculty felt that the administration held them between a rock and a hard place — or, perhaps more clearly, held them to impossible expectations. Many, certainly, came to believe that their efforts in the several critical areas of minority initiatives were not being appreciated.

Faculty searches, according to those in the trenches doing the nitty-gritty work — the letter writing, placing ads, telephoning, attending meetings to interview prospective candidates — went to great lengths to find qualified minority candidates. Faculty believed their efforts were conscientious, sustained, and went well beyond the ordinary, traditional kind of faculty search. Some in the administration came to believe, however, that "the faculty were dragging their feet," at the very least implying a less than conscientious effort. At worst, some believed they were being accused of a racist bias and of attitudes that were seriously damaging to the larger diversity interests of the campus. The effort to bring in minority faculty and to recruit and retain minority students had become contentious.

The Flint Campus was experiencing in microcosm the much larger, seemingly intractable, American social crisis: the crisis rooted in the varied perceptions and realities of racism. It was and remains a seemingly intractable crisis in that blacks see whites caught up in self deception about what is, in fact, a persistent racial prejudice. They see equal opportunity as little more than a thin facade concealing an insidious structure of discrimination. On the other side whites see a widening field of opportunity that blacks have failed to use to full advantage. They see charges of racism as largely unfair and unwarranted. Charges of discrimination on the one side give rise to charges of reverse discrimination on the other. The climate is one of skepticism, to say the least, of the one group about the good intentions and credibility of the other. The University of Michigan–Flint came to mirror certain elements in this larger issue. A little understanding and empathy from the one side for the other, and a commitment from both sides to reasonable discussion proceeding from the shared values of an academic community, should have precluded a collision on minority initiatives at the Flint Campus. It didn't happen that way.

The Flint Campus Issue

The specific issue was minority recruitment. The faculty, in point of fact, were faced with a real scarcity of minority candidates. The difficulties in all of those faculty searches were compounded by the relatively few numbers of minorities with Ph.D.s or other appropriate credentials in the fields being searched, and by the high demand nationwide from what in fact was a small pool of candidates. This was true in all fields, but in some like the natural sciences it meant that coming up with a pool of candidates for interviewing that would include a minority was virtually impossible. The Flint Campus was competing with nearly every college and university across the country — at one time or another — for the few qualified minorities available.

Eventually there was a moment of confrontation between the faculty and the Chancellor on the issues of minority recruitment and progress in securing greater diversity within the Flint Campus community. Some in the administration, wearying of what they perceived as at the very least not very helpful faculty attitudes, were of a mind to simply say to the faculty, in effect: "If you're not with us (on these issues), then get out of the way. We'll deal with these matters without you!"

There are, of course, different perceptions of who was at fault and what had gone wrong. Some faculty believed that while comments from some administrators had been intemperate, the Chancellor had been essentially correct in his assessment of an uncooperative, unwilling and sometimes obstructionist faculty. Others, perhaps the greater number, felt that faculty efforts to increase the numbers of minorities on the campus, and secure real diversity, had been both persistent and substantial. They were offended by statements and suggestions to the contrary. They were bewildered — some even angered — by the expression of administrative views on these matters.

What followed was a bit of self-righteous public posturing on both sides, including news stories and a full page ad in *The Flint Journal* affirming community support for Chancellor Jones. In the end nothing was really resolved, though the campus did find itself eventually moving beyond what had been a few weeks of strident rhetoric.

The damage from such confrontations, when there is no meeting of minds and no clearing of the air with reasoned discussion, is a serious matter. While the periodic collision of faculty and administrative perspectives is often the very stuff of a healthy academic community, this collision left a few major dents. In the best of times there is resolution and the community of learning, the student-faculty enterprise, is infused with newfound energy and common goals and purposes are rediscovered. In the worst of times, some damage is sustained and a campus then has to go on with its business, with matters largely unresolved and a few bruises evident, to face new issues and to perhaps recast the old ones in new circumstances.

In this particular instance, it was believed by many faculty that numbers of administrators had come to the conclusion that significant parts of the minority-diversity agenda would have to be pursued without the faculty. If there was any substance to this belief, the danger was that some parts of the administration were finding it convenient to forget that it is the faculty and the students together in an environment supportive of learning that centers and defines a campus community. Important things are simply not accomplished without that "defining center." Others found it convenient to forget what "shared governance" was all about.

One symptom of the problem was the increasing tendency on campus to leave "faculty" out of the student-faculty equation, and simply say about the mission of the campus that "we are here for the students!", which is but part of the picture. This sort of rhetoric had become common by 1995. What such statements do, of course, is diminish the defining role of a faculty and, at least on some matters, to assert a primary, sometimes preemptive role for others in a broad range of decision making in areas of traditional concern to the faculty.

And, On Another Front, Some Strategic Planning!

A major development in these years, perhaps inspired by the Michigan Mandate of President Duderstadt in Ann Arbor, was a new strategic planning effort, initiated by Chancellor Jones in January, 1988. This Strategic Planning Committee, chaired by Professor Peter Gluck (Political Science), produced an ambitious and comprehensive planning document with the significant title "Partnership for Progress." The idea of "partnership" was central. The Gluck Committee recommended a whole series of initiatives designed, in the words of the final report, "to strengthen the tradition of partnership between liberal education and professional studies and between the University and the region it serves."

The Mission Statement drafted by the Committee reiterated and expanded upon earlier campus statements as to purposes and goals. While elsewhere the strategic planning document addressed minority initiatives and diversity, the Mission Statement focused on the following: "that a coherent liberal education is the core of the academic enterprise"; that The University of Michigan–Flint is "an institution in which excellence in teaching is especially important and emphasis is placed on learning"; where there is a commitment to expand "opportunities for access to and participation in higher education by traditional and non-traditional students"; and where "educational partnership embracing . . . faculty, staff and students," and the traditions and procedures of "shared governance" are valued.

This Mission Statement appeared to give particular emphasis to the need to articulate a campus spirit of partnership, especially between the College of Arts and Sciences on the one hand, and the two professional schools on the other: the School of Management and the School of Health Professions and Studies. More expansively, the academic community was to be enhanced by the further pursuit of partnership among the major segments of the campus community: students, faculty, and staff. This was clearly an important need. Second, the Mission Statement pointed to a broader range of community and regional responsibilities than had been articulated in earlier documents. What was new in this regard was a greater sense of immediacy and urgency.

The Strategic Plan itself contained specific proposals for virtually every area of campus life, though the focus was clearly on academic concerns. The document called for an evaluation of general education requirements, the development of an "outcomes assessment of learning" process, and for some specific goal and action plans intended to enhance "a pluralistic environment."

Progress was to occur in some of these areas, while little was to be seen in others. A major concern, following the submission of "Partnership in Progress," was that there were no clear understandings or agreement on how and when the Plan was to be implemented. For whatever the reason, some proposals were apparently "dead in the water" rather early. The following stand as a few good examples: the proposal that there be stronger ties between WFUM-TV (Channel 28) and academic programs; the proposal that there be a Dean for the School of Health Professions and Studies; that there be graduate programs in Education and in an interdisciplinary applied science program; that there be support for staff development; and that there be a tripling of the size of the library collection (to achieve parity with peer institutions).

On the one hand there was an obvious scarcity of resources with which to implement some of the more significant parts of this planning document; on the other there was an apparent lack of interest in assigning priorities and developing a detailed implementation strategy — which, of course, would have led to a clear delineation of what was to be pursued and what was not. That did not happen.

One further part of the "Partnership in Progress" document requires at least brief discussion. In the section titled "External Relations" the plan called for two primary directions of effort. The first was a focus on the Project for Urban and Regional Affairs (PURA), thereby giving primary emphasis on research and technical support of regional economic development. The other focus was to be on the programs and activities of the Office of Extension and Continuing Education, primarily on non-credit courses that address retraining needs in the region. With both PURA and Extension The University of Michigan–Flint was to bring its resources and expertise to bear on economic and development problems facing Flint, Genesee County, and the larger region served by the campus.

The Project for Urban and Regional Affairs was set up in 1984. Under the sustained direction of Alice Hart, PURA has been an exemplary model of the varying ways the resources and talents available in higher education can be given application in a diverse urban and regional environment. The advantages have worked both ways, in the case of the Flint Campus. Flint and the surrounding areas have benefited in measurable ways by having access to research and technical support from the University. The University gains by accruing validity to its assertion of the value of applied research (alongside the more "traditional" forms of faculty research) in such everyday, practical matters as tenure, promotion and merit salary increases. The University also gains in being able to provide students who are assisting faculty with research with a valuable internship experience. Finally, as one observer noted, "there is being accumulated a rich resource in information about the community", information about environmental quality, public opinion on a range of current issues, health and housing matters, transportation, the arts, issues concerning the aged, employment patterns, and much more. PURA remains a very important and quickly identifiable interface of campus and the region it serves.

Before looking at Extension and Continuing Education, it is appropriate to take a step forward to the more recent past and say something briefly about the Community Stabilization and Revitalization Project (CSR), a grant-funded outreach program which began in early 1994. With different emphases and focus than PURA, CSR also has emphasized the principle of university-community partnership, a major point in the Gluck Strategic Plan. PURA and CSR together came to constitute the most prominent of a growing number of linkages with the community. The CSR, under the direction of Kristen Skivington and with a staff which included John Coleman, Renee Zientek, and Pat Mansour, has provided technical assistance and counseling to the area's business community and non-profit organizations.

In its first eighteen months CSR provided a range of such advice and technical assistance. About 75% of the consultants used on the 45 projects in that time were University of Michigan–Flint faculty and staff. CSR project manager John Coleman summed up the program's mission with the comment "We weave ourselves into the community by tapping our professors' expertise. We want the community to look to the university to find people who can assist them." In terms of general mission, CSR and PURA share some common ground.

Largely grant funded, the life of CSR was extended in 1995 by a grant from the U.S. Department of Education. Two factors helped secure the grant. First, The University of Michigan–Flint was given federal designation as an urban university; and second, the city's successful effort in 1994 to have the Flint area designated as an enterprise community zone. Flint's mayor Woodrow Stanley, Congressman Dale Kildee, and Flint Community Development Executive Director Bobby Wells all agreed that the 1994 Enterprise Zone grant smoothed the way for the 1995 CSR funding. It was expected that this partnership would lead to yet further federal monies finding their way into the Flint area economy. A great deal depended, of course, on prospects for continued funding for CSR.

The Office of Extension and Continuing Education, in one form or another, has a long history in the Flint area. An Office of Graduate Extension was established in Flint in 1944, the initial presence of The University of Michigan in Flint. That office continued to function for some years after the establishment of the Flint College as a separately administered operation. Its operation was substantial. By the late 1960s about a thousand graduate course registrations occurred each semester, and Flint faculty taught many of those courses. With the transition from college to regional university campus, the extension and continuing education operations were placed under the singular administrative authority of the Chancellor.

In effect, after 1974 or so, the Office of Extension and Continuing Education had a reduced and redefined role. Graduate courses, in the main, were to be offered by the College of Arts and Sciences (the MLS Program in American Culture and the MPA Program in Public Administration) or by the School of Management (the MBA Program). Non-credit instruction was to be the primary focus of the Office of Extension. There were some years, when Doug Kelley served as Director in the 1980s, when enthusiasm and energy produced an impressive number of course offerings and a highly visible Office of Continuing Education.

The absence of base budget funding for most of the Continuing Education and Extension programs was a major problem. Coordinating those course offerings with what might be called faculty interests and administrative exigencies was yet another source of occasional difficulty. A planning document in the early 1980s, in some ways anticipating the 1988 "Partnership for Progress," called for funding and other support that would considerably enhance the place of continuing education on campus. Optimistically, that document called for an extension and continuing education operation that would exist for the institution as a "third arm," the other two being the undergraduate and graduate programs offered by The University of Michigan–Flint.

Little has occurred since 1988 to suggest that, with PURA and CSR, the Office of Extension and Continuing Education might significantly address "retraining needs in the region." The problem, perhaps as is always the case, is principally the tangled one of resources, funding, support, and personnel. This part of academic affairs continues to be an under-developed and disappointingly low-profile area of University of Michigan–Flint activity.

The Academic Advising Center

New developments (other than PURA) were to occur before the strategic planning effort of 1988. Among them one of the most important was the establishment of an Academic Advising Center, which has been under the sustained direction of Lora Beckwith since its inception in 1986. Increased enrollments, the increased complexity of a multi-unit campus, and the inability or unwillingness of faculty to carry the full load of advising finally led to the establishment, in Academic Affairs, of this center.

There had been at least one intermediary step. Somewhat earlier, in the 1970s, Ron Wisner created "The FACTory," an advising resource in Student Services which with very limited means provided needed support to what was then entirely a faculty advising operation. Even that needs qualification. A number of professional staff, mainly in Student Services, had also served as advisors in those early years, some with fairly heavy advising responsibilities. Interestingly, in 1995 the Advising Center was once again placed, for administrative purposes, in Student Services.

From the faculty perspective an advising center was needed due to the increased number of students with concentration interests, those students enrolled in departmental programs. The faculty believed that newly admitted students, transfer students, and others who had not yet decided upon a major would be best advised in a center designed and equipped specifically for that purpose. There were other contributing factors as well. By the 1980s, if not earlier, significant numbers of faculty were living some distance from Flint, more were spending less time than in earlier years on campus and were therefore less accessible to the larger number of students, and — not the least — faculty were under increased pressure to do more research, writing, and other categories of accomplishment that fall under the heading of professional development. For all of that, it is likely that an academic advising center that could provide high quality, consistent, accessible advising and academic information to the thousands of freshmen, transfer students, and others not yet formally in a particular academic program would be a necessity when the campus attained a certain enrollment plateau.

More than thirty-five faculty have had appointments in the Advising Center. These faculty have attended special training sessions so that they might respond knowledgeably to students' questions and interests. Their appointments have been yearly; some are half-time, some full-time (involving 75 or 150 hours of advising obligation). With their appointments, the Advising Center has attempted to represent "diversity of discipline, gender, race, and experience at the University."

Undoubtedly because of the quality and dedication of the people involved, the Academic Advising Center has been a highly successful aspect of the University's academic operations. One can safely assume this given the fact that, first, its task of telling students what courses to take and, by inference, what not to take, make it a fine target for faculty criticism; and, second, there have indeed been few complaints. When there have been problems it was usually because a department or a faculty member did not make clear some point about prerequisites, or there was a failure in getting information from one place to another.

The current assumption is that the Advising Center will continue to serve students and faculty with the same high quality after its 1995 move from Academic Affairs to Student Services. Most believe that it matters rather little where the unit is administratively housed; it matters greatly who runs it.

To Organize or Not?
Collective Bargaining and a Faculty Union

A major faculty issue and, rather soon, a wider campus and University issue, was whether the faculty should organize for collective bargaining. While this question had been raised from time to time in earlier years, it was not until 1989 that Professor Tom Coffey (Social Work) gave some focus to an increased faculty interest in organizing for collective bargaining.

That interest was initially mobilized through a series of regularly scheduled Saturday morning meetings of ten to fifteen faculty who gathered at Churchill's, a pub in downtown Flint. This early group established itself as a UAW Organizing Group, believing that faculty interests would best be served with this affiliation. It was Tom Coffey's initiative and sustained efforts that gave cohesion and direction to the early stages of these efforts.

The push for faculty collective bargaining, beginning in 1989, was the consequence of three circumstances. First, there was a growing unease among faculty that the principle of shared governance, in which faculty and administration would work together in coming to important decisions, was no longer operative.

Faculty had come to believe that committees working with key administrators had no more than advisory functions and that, even in that role, they were often informed after the fact of decisions already taken. In the words of some, the faculty had been gradually "peripheralized" — removed from any significant role in the making of important decisions. Those decisions were seen as having a direct and immediate bearing on the academic concerns of the faculty and on the learning environment of the campus, in which faculty had legitimate and primary interest.

The role of an advisory committee was, therefore, only a reactive one, not a participatory one. Committee members often found themselves simply trying to get information, trying to find out what decisions had been made or were about to be made. Administrators, for their part, usually argued that in fact there had been appropriate consultation, that information had been made available in a timely manner, and that faculty were too often insensitive to the pressure of events and circumstances in which administrators were expected to function.

Second, there were concerns about what was happening to the "academic quality" of the University, and what might be in store for the future should the faculty not devise some more effective means of addressing the issue. While not all faculty agreed, those involved saw faculty collective bargaining as a necessary means of strengthening the traditions and procedures of shared governance in ways that would assure the enhancement of academic quality at The University of Michigan–Flint.

Its advocates also saw faculty collective bargaining as the appropriate means of assuring both administrative accountability and the accessibility of information, especially budgetary and financial information. They believed that, if the academic community was to sustain and even enhance a high quality learning environment, then a better system of administrative accountability and access to budget information must be secured. These were the most frequently expressed arguments by those faculty who felt that union organizing and collective bargaining had become a necessity.

There were, of course, other issues as well. The steadily growing reliance on part-time faculty, as a way of cutting costs — a situation over which the faculty felt it had no control — was a continuing source of major concern. It was believed that collective bargaining would directly involve faculty in this area. Faculty salaries and benefits were also an issue. While critics of the organizing effort suggested that faculty salaries were the overriding interest, those involved in the organizing effort were quick to respond that the principal motivation was concern about academic quality; salary and benefits matters were important insofar as they believed that The University of Michigan–Flint must remain competitive with peer institutions if the campus was going to be able to attract and retain a high quality faculty.

While the organizing movement gained momentum and in time secured support from more than half of the faculty, some remained opposed. While the reasons were often individual, there were a least a few common denominators that defined the opposition. Some believed that any organizing effort would inevitably undermine or somehow compromise existing structures and procedures for faculty governance. They argued that the thing to do was to fix what wasn't working well, if indeed that proved to be the case, rather than to supplant it with something else. That something else — a union — they believed to be quite alien to the traditions of a University of Michigan faculty. That truly was important to them. It simply was not appropriate for a University of Michigan faculty to organize a union.

Second, there were those who believed that a successful establishment of a faculty collective bargaining unit on the Flint Campus would place in jeopardy or at the very least raise unwanted questions about the relationship with the Ann Arbor campus. Put bluntly, would a faculty union on the Flint Campus lead first President Duderstadt and then the Regents to consider the separation of the Flint Campus from the University system?

There were also those who believed that, all the rhetoric aside, the real issue was faculty salaries: a demand for more money at a time when the University was faced with scarce resources and could only accommodate bargained-for faculty salary increases by raising student tuition and fees. And, finally, more as an attitude than a specific point of objection, some faculty likely believed that union organizing was simply an inappropriate behavior for faculty professionals. Whatever the problems, and there were of course disagreements on the nature and extent of those problems, other means than "union organizing" should be found to resolve them.

One very probable area of faculty agreement in all of this discussion, not always expressed in the open forum of a faculty meeting, though often the stuff of faculty conversation in offices or over a cup of coffee, was concern about "academic quality." While faculty have always been dismayed that too many students show up in their classes ill-prepared for the tasks before them, and are on occasion dismayed by an administration with apparently ill-advised priorities and policies, these areas of dismay had deepened into something more than the usual complaints by 1989.

The AAUP (American Association of University Professors) expressed anxiety about academic quality was symptomatic of a wider sense that relatively recent developments in higher education threatened both academic quality and credibility. What had course grades, and even the baccalaureate degree, come to really mean? Were students really getting what could be called a rigorous and meaningful education? How well, and adequately, were large numbers of them being taught? How did it come about that other institutional concerns had taken precedence over learning? Were those much talked about "scarce resources" being used wisely and appropriately to further learning, the student-faculty enterprise, on campus? Or were resources being pre-empted in ways that would have the eventual consequence of diminishing academic quality? How about the numbers of students who lacked even the basic reading, writing, quantitative and perhaps even the kind of disciplined thinking skills necessary to university level work? What, responsibly, could be done for them? Who in the administration was really listening to faculty concerns?

How, indeed, was academic quality to be measured on a campus like that of The University of Michigan–Flint? Was some new yardstick required? Would new measures of quality be anything other than ill-concealed default from the standards by which most faculty had come to measure academic quality — an understanding that for many went back two, three, and for some, four decades? These were increasingly worrisome questions in the decade of the 1980s— more worrisome, certainly, than anything that might easily be dismissed as simply "the usual faculty griping."

The roots of this worry about a decline in academic quality can be found at least a decade earlier. It was probably there no later than the mid-1970s. This concern was and remains common to much of higher education across the country. The Flint Campus faculty organizing effort was but one local expression of that concern.

As discussions continued in 1990 and 1991 a decision was made to explore organizing alternatives to the UAW. As it turned out there were two such alternatives: the American Association of University Professors (AAUP) and the Michigan Education Association (MEA). In the spring of 1991 a ballot was taken and it was determined that the AAUP would be the organizing representative. The organizing campus leadership by this time included Nathan Oaklander (Philosophy), Peggy Kahn (Political Science), Chuck Dunlop (Philosophy), Carl Rinne (Education) and Frank Richardson (Foreign Languages). Clearly the larger numbers supporting this effort were found in the College of Arts and Sciences; fewer were found from the School of Management or from the School of Health Professions and Studies.

In the winter of 1992 nearly 65% of the faculty indicated that they wished to have an election to determine whether or not there would be collective bargaining on the Flint Campus. Until this time the administration in Ann Arbor had been silent. But with this expression of faculty opinion on the Flint Campus, they took exception — arguing that the Flint Campus was not a separate unit (for such purposes) and therefore an election could not be held unless the appropriate percentage of the entire three campus (Ann Arbor, Dearborn, and Flint) faculty of nearly 5,000 were all involved.

What followed was a long, drawn-out legal confrontation. It began in September 1992 when the Flint AAUP Chapter, financially supported by the Michigan Conference of the AAUP and the National AAUP, argued its case before the Michigan Employment Relations Commission (MERC). Nathan Oaklander (Philosophy), Bill Lockwood (English), and Bob Bix (Mathematics) — speaking for the Flint AAUP — argued that a range of differences in employment (salary, course load, expectations in employment), different Flint Campus circumstances than prevailed in Ann Arbor, and the fact of a separate state appropriation for Flint all suggested that Flint should justifiably be treated as a separate unit on this issue. Ann Arbor representatives argued the point that the Flint Campus was in every consequential way an integral part of a single University system. The Flint AAUP lost the case.

An important point surfaced as a consequence of this collective bargaining initiative. From time to time in recent years there has been the occasional question and comment about the possibility of the Flint Campus going its own way, altogether separate as a state institution. Almost everyone in Flint, in Genesee County, in the surrounding areas, and in the campus community believed that The University of Michigan–Flint should continue as an integral and important part of the three campus system of The University of Michigan. Those who argued differently were both short-sighted and wrong-headed. Continuing as an integral part of The University of Michigan system was a fundamental premise from which most thinking proceeded on any matter relating to the Flint Campus. That point had held for forty years. Those who argued for collective bargaining had not questioned that premise. They had, however, insisted that certain differing circumstances warranted Flint being regarded separately for the *singular* purposes of organizing a faculty union.

Ann Arbor and, in particular, President Duderstadt were found arguing for an integral system in every consequential regard, thereby giving affirmation to the Ann Arbor–Flint connection and to the continuance of a three campus system with no campus going its separate way, least of all on the matter of faculty collective bargaining.

Upon later consultation with Michigan and National AAUP officials, the Flint AAUP decided to appeal the MERC Board ruling. The case was heard by the Michigan Court of Appeals in May of 1995. Later that year, in September, the Court of Appeals upheld the MERC decision, arguing that all University of Michigan campuses constituted essentially one university and therefore should be regarded as one faculty group. The decision came as no surprise at the Flint Campus — either to the faculty or to the administration.

In a more general sense, the surfacing and pursuit of this issue has been indicative of unresolved issues on the Flint Campus that are rooted in concerns about academic quality, the role of faculty, and the traditions and procedures of faculty governance. Whether or not the appointment of a new Chancellor, Dr. Charlie Nelms, in 1994, and the administrative changes in 1995 and 1996, would sufficiently improve faculty-administration relations and enable these issues to be addressed in a constructive manner remains to be seen. More on that in the last chapter of this book. It is probably safe to imagine, however, that even as this book goes to press, the jury will still be out.

In the meantime, campus AAUP leadership saw in the Court of Appeals decision an opportunity to address a broad range of specific matters for the faculty at Flint, including professional development opportunities, new leverage on salary matters, and a more effective relationship with the administration. For its part the administration saw no significant changes coming from the Appeals Court decision. In the short term, the AAUP Chapter remained alive and well on the Flint Campus, pursued its on-going agenda, and undertook to expand its membership. As of September 1995, 55 of 190 full-time faculty were AAUP members. The AAUP Chapter also continued its regular meetings with counterparts on the Dearborn and Ann Arbor campuses.

The Riverfront Campus, 1995

Campus Expansion:
The Thompson Library and the University Pavilion

A major concern for the entire campus community, one that had hung over the university like a cloud for several decades, was the continuing absence of a library building. Those faculty for whom a library was the most important campus resource were especially eager that a fully developed library be available. It was to finally happen.

A major accomplishment of the administration of Clinton Jones was to secure the financing, building, and completion of the Frances Willson Thompson Library. At long last! The Thompson Library, which was opened in 1994, stands as a beautifully designed and architecturally elegant addition to the Flint Campus. It has clearly become the crown jewel of the campus.

The Thompson Library was a very long time in coming. More than one member of the campus community in those intervening years was to remark that it was extraordinary that a campus of The University of Michigan — or of any college or university for that matter — would allow *thirty-eight* years to pass before securing a real library. After all, isn't the library, with the faculty, the principal resource of an academic community? In fairness, the absence of a real library building probably should be dated from 1977, the year of the move to the Riverfront Campus.

The emphasis should be on the word "real." In one form or another a library had existed since the early days of the Flint College. For a time "the library" consisted of a small collection housed in a classroom in the Mott Memorial Building. Then there was the Mott Library, a shared facility and collection with the Community College. That arrangement was to last until the move to the Riverfront Campus and the completion of the Classroom Office Building (CROB) in 1977. Until that year there was at least the sense of a library resource and of a building which was "the library." With the move downtown, the combined Mott Library collection was uncomfortably split and University of Michigan–Flint titles were moved to the fifth floor of CROB. Even then, until engineers gave their nod of approval, there was a moment of anxiety that other arrangements would have to be made for the collection. The fear was that the structure had not been designed to handle the weight of a library collection on the entire fifth floor.

Once the fifth floor of CROB was deemed structurally sufficient to the task, it became the temporary housing for the library, its collections and its staff. It was not long, however, before a significant quantity of titles had to be placed in storage, some in the basement of the Hubbard Building, which housed Plant Services and Campus Safety. The optimism that the temporary facility was indeed temporary was evident in the search for a librarian who would be involved in the planning and construction of a library building for the Riverfront Campus. David Palmer was hired with that goal very much in mind. The idea in those years was that the state of Michigan could be persuaded to appropriate sufficient monies for a library building. This did not turn out to be the case.

A number of years were to pass, the "interregnum" as we have called it, during which hopes for state funding dimmed. The word "temporary" assumed a new meaning, especially for the library staff. In the meantime, the library spilled over into the ground floor level of the Harrison Street Parking Ramp. Some refurbished space at the street level allowed for needed shelving and files for the growing collection of United States Government Documents, a growing University and local history archives, and an assortment of other materials including thousands of volumes of books and periodicals for which there was no room on the fifth floor of CROB.

For those who from time to time thought much about it — and the library staff confronted it every day — the absence of a library building was an embarrassment. Here was a regional campus of The University of Michigan trying to provide essential resources and services to both students and faculty for an increasingly diverse number of undergraduate and graduate programs. Inter-library loans and the resources of libraries on the Ann Arbor campus some fifty five miles distant neither diminished the difficulties nor alleviated the embarrassment.

When it became clear that state appropriations would not be forthcoming, Chancellor Jones undertook to raise private monies for the library. Joanne Sullenger, Vice Chancellor for Development, had a key role and deserves considerable credit for her success in fund raising for the library and, it should be said, for raising considerable other monies as well. The beginnings of a campus endowment fund by Chancellor Moran in the 1970s provided a threshold for the later library fund raising effort. Contributions specifically for the library were obtained from many sources, with several exceptionally generous donors — most especially Dr. and Mrs. Jack Willson Thompson — making the entire project eventually possible. So, finally in 1994, The University of Michigan–Flint became a campus with a REAL library. The opening of the Frances Willson Thompson Library has given the campus a sense of completeness, a sense of having attained sufficient critical mass in terms of essential physical facilities to see itself as a developed campus.

In recent years the library's acquisitions budget has grown substantially. While efforts to build its collections continue, the library has significantly augmented its resources by way of computer linkages to the catalogs and collections of a number of local and more distant academic libraries. A major problem facing the library in recent years has been that of staff shortages. Its professional staff have been stretched thin, and relief is required in order for the new facility and its resources to be optimally utilized. These problems should be resolved as resources become available. In the meantime, the addition of the Thompson Library stands as a major accomplishment of the administration of Clinton Jones.

Changing the Face of the Fortress

A long-standing concern of Chancellor Jones, and of others in the campus community, was the seemingly fortress-like presence of the Riverfront Campus adjoining the downtown area. The complex of brick buildings and the way in which the campus plan had evolved from the mid-1970s had the apparent effect of somehow distancing university facilities and the campus community from the Flint community. That was the impression the walls of brick building apparently conveyed. A fortress! Although altogether unintended, the appearance could be seen as somehow unfriendly — a campus certainly right there adjoining the downtown, but nonetheless remote!

The opportunity to acquire the Waterstreet Pavilion, located a block to the west on Saginaw Street, gave the campus an opportunity to address this perception. The background to the University's acquisition of the Pavilion is significant in that it was only when one of the City of Flint's efforts at downtown revitalization went awry that the property became available to the University. When that happened the campus had a different physical presence in the downtown area.

The Waterstreet Pavilion had been part of an ambitious downtown development, which included a Hyatt Hotel (now a Radisson Hotel) and, just across the Flint River, a theme park: Autoworld. Autoworld, a celebration of the automobile industry, was intended to be a major tourist attraction. Convention facilities, a theme park and the Pavilion collectively were to be the combined catalyst for the revival of Flint's downtown, a revival that would bring both retail businesses and people back to the downtown area. It didn't happen. In fact, it became more and more clear (to some at least) that the downtown would be increasingly defined by the presence of the University campus, by city and county government facilities, by the banks, and by the local newspaper. To increasing numbers it appeared unlikely that there would be a significant return of retail and other businesses to the downtown area. The short term future of Flint's downtown, at the least, would be differently defined. The University would become a major part of that definition.

The University Pavilion

Waterstreet Pavilion then became the University Pavilion, an architecturally varied and attractive facility with adjoining parking decks. On its main floor are found an information area, the campus bookstore and a range of food vendors. On the second floor are located University administrative offices and the Academic Advising Center. Enclosed elevated walkways, the most recent one crossing just above Harrison Street, have allowed all those concerned about traffic, inclement weather — or those who just like to stay inside — access to virtually every corner of the Riverfront Campus, from the Pavilion, to the Thompson Library, to CROB, to the Murchie Science Building, to the University Center. On the east side of the campus the Recreation Building is connected to the University Center. The planned University acquisition of the defunct Autoworld property across the river and, possibly some day, the State Office Building just to the north of the University

Pavilion, will enable an even more expansive downtown presence for the campus and a further challenge to those who design enclosed and elevated walkways.

Until the Pavilion was acquired by the University, the Chancellor, the Provost and a number of other administrators, including the Director of Admissions and the Registrar, had been located in CROB. The proximity of these administrators to faculty, classrooms, and students was important at a time when serious issues and problems were having the effect of distancing administrators, faculty, and staff. Crossing Harrison Street to the Pavilion to find these administrators was not a matter of traversing some great distance. There was, however, no longer the visibility, the easy accessibility, of these administrative offices once they were relocated in the Pavilion.

The Women's Center

Among the initial occupants of the University Pavilion were the staff of the Adult Resource Center and of the Women's Center. While the Women's Center was new, the Adult Resource Center was the new name given to the Re-entry Center. The new name was intended to better reflect what in fact the Re-entry Center had been doing for nearly fifteen years: providing assistance and encouragement to undergraduate adult students (age 22 and older) throughout their years at the Flint campus, and not just at the point of admission or return. Both the Adult Resource Center and the Women's Center, staffed by Jan Worth and Peggy Holcomb, were set up to function under the general administrative oversight of Lora Beckwith, the Director of the Academic Advising Center.

Student demographics made clear a necessary and close association of the Adult Resource Center and the Women's Center. Significant changes had taken place over a fifteen year period. Adult students (22 or older) constituted 33% of the student body by 1976; by 1990 that percentage had almost doubled, to 62%. The reasons were clear. Both the pool and the numbers of traditional-age students (18 to 21) locally and nationally had declined dramatically. Equally important, there were increasing numbers of new students transferring from the community colleges and other institutions, as well as sustained numbers of older students either returning to complete an interrupted education or perhaps to begin their higher education. It was noted, as well, that over 60% of the students were women, and about 40% of *all* students were women who were 22 years old or older. The new programs were designed to respond to the new demographic realities as well as to address issues specific to women's concerns.

The Women's Center was set up to maintain and develop the resources appropriate to what women's centers had become on campuses across the country. The Center was intended to provide advising and counseling support to women students, to represent the interests of women to the administration and other campus decision makers, and to network with other women's organizations and groups both in the community and beyond. The Center also provides staff support and space for Women's History Month activities and events and administers the

Dorothea Wyatt Award. This award, which since 1989 has annually celebrated the achievements and contributions of outstanding women faculty and staff members, has been a particularly distinctive way in which the campus has recognized the centrally important role of women faculty and staff in the life of the campus community.

Both the Adult Resource Center and the Women's Center have provided support and services well beyond what their rather limited staff and budget might suggest. One continuing problem is that too few women faculty have devoted time and interest to such tasks as program planning for Women's History Month. The programs and activities of the Center are outstanding in spite of this problem.

A Multiple-Unit Campus

This narrative portrait does not encompass an attempt at a broad description of the academic programs, schools, or the several faculties which comprise The University of Michigan–Flint. A few general comments about how the multiple units came about are, however, in order. As we have noted, the Flint College at its inception was essentially an arts and sciences faculty offering a single baccalaureate degree. The Business Administration and Education Departments were staffed by just a few faculty, and the single unit organization of the early Flint College was maintained for almost two decades. There was a certain irony in this, as almost from the outset most students were enrolled in either business administration or in elementary or secondary teacher certificate programs in education.

The *Haber Report,* in 1969, anticipated that business and management faculty and their programs would be separated, thereby becoming a distinct school (the School of Management) with its own dean and its own degrees. That happened in 1975. There was some thought that Education, which had remained a department in the College of Arts and Sciences, would soon follow suit. For reasons about which everyone has a different opinion, that has never happened. What did happen was that a third unit emerged as a result of the coalescence of several programs in health sciences.

It was through the relocation of the Physical Therapy Program from the Ann Arbor campus to the Flint campus in 1982 — a rare opportunity seized upon by Chancellor Conny Nelson — that a third academic unit was established. Initially called the School of Health Sciences, it soon became the School of Health Professions and Studies (SHPS) in 1989. The several programs and departments that comprise the school retained a good deal of authority, each with its own director. In this regard it differed from the other two units. The administrative concerns of the school reside with a coordinator. Health Care, Medical Technology, Nursing (a BSN program), Anesthesia (a M.S. program) and Physical Therapy (a master's program) are the principal programs of the school.

Some of these programs, such as Medical Technology and Nursing, had been around for several years. In the case of Nursing, the School of Nursing in Ann Arbor had initial administrative and degree granting responsibility for the program. The transition to a program fully located at the Flint Campus was later complicated by seemingly endless discussions and negotiations with the Hurley Medical Center regarding its School of Nursing. There were exploratory discussions about a possible combined Hurley-Flint College nursing program as early as 1966.

What occurred — finally — in the early 1990s was a phasing out of the Hurley School of Nursing, with its last class graduating in December of 1995. The two-year Hurley Nursing program was incorporated into the Flint Campus BSN Program in Nursing. The Hurley School of Nursing, founded in 1909, had served the area for 86 years as the major regional institution for nursing education and training. In 1995 the combined program officially became The University of Michigan–Flint/Hurley BSN Program.

Ellen Woodman, long-time director of the Flint Campus Nursing Program, was to see that evolution and negotiation through its frequently difficult and always bewildering rites of passage. The tasks were sequential: to secure separation from the School of Nursing on the Ann Arbor campus, to define the place of the Nursing Program on the Flint Campus and within the School of Health Professions and Studies, to develop the BSN program, and to help bring to fruition the seemingly endless, sometimes hopelessly stalled negotiations with Hurley Medical Center.

The establishment of the School of Health Professions and Studies occasioned a fundamental and, for some, long overdue re-structuring of general education requirements. As we have noted, from its beginnings as the Flint College to later years with the College of Arts and Sciences, it was the arts and sciences faculty which had full responsibility for the determination, instruction, and administration of the general education requirements for all undergraduate degrees at the Flint Campus.

The continuing growth of the two other units, Management and Health Professions and Studies, was the occasion for change. One of the most effective advocates for that change was Richard Darnell, the first director of the Physical Therapy Program. The argument was rather clear and simple. It was also in keeping with the Bylaws of the Regents of the University. The determination of course and degree requirements, including those which would fall under the heading of general education, is the province of the academic unit, of the faculty granting the degree. As it has developed, decisions as to requirements, courses and credits now are separately the concern of the three academic units, while most of the actual instruction in general education courses has remained with the faculty of the College of Arts and Sciences.

A diminished role for the College of Arts and Sciences in general education — bemoaned by some, celebrated by others — was an inevitable and probably overdue consequence of the earlier transition from the Flint College to a university campus, a multi-unit University of Michigan–Flint. The Regents' Bylaws were clear.

The new challenge, or if not new then one cast in a different form, was to develop a sense of partnership and scholarly community which would have meaning and substance for the faculties of the three units. The problem is a general one in higher education. Multiple unit universities are by definition organized into schools and colleges, each with its own traditions, each a community unto itself. The task then becomes one of identifying and securing the common ground shared by all. Reaffirming the centrality of the arts and sciences, of the principles of a liberal education on a university campus, is central to that task. The idea of "partnership" found in the *Strategic Plan* (1989) addressed this need for the Flint Campus.

The Harding Mott University Center

The Passing Present

The most recent phase of this "work in progress" has been marked by further change. Not surprising! By the mid-1990s new faces along with a collection of retirements, resignations, and people otherwise going on to do other things were re-defining The University of Michigan–Flint to a degree perhaps unprecedented in the nearly forty-year history of the campus.

It is likely that new people even more than new circumstances in the past five to ten years have been at the root of that re-definition. In the early years, the 1960s and the 1970s, new people, both faculty and staff, were largely absorbed by the campus culture, by already largely established patterns, values, and perceptions. This has been far less the case in more recent years. A growing number of faculty and staff retirements since the mid-1980s, a larger and more impersonal institution, administrative agenda quite different from that of earlier years, more clearly articulated community expectations, and the arrival of new people with different interests, priorities, and agenda have all had consequences. Certainly the retirement of twenty-five senior faculty in the years from 1988 - 1995 marked major changes in faculty leadership and in the profile of the Governing Faculty. Yet which of these several factors was most important would be difficult to determine. A good guess might point to both new people and administrative agenda!

Whereas earlier "metamorphoses" of the campus were largely structural and programmatic, the metamorphosis experienced in the last ten years (before 1996) was more fundamental. These more recent changes had more to do with less tangibly objective institutional characteristics. They were the consequences of the way in which individuals perceived their particular places and roles in the larger campus community. Obviously, institutions of higher learning don't stand still, at least not for very long. The Flint Campus has been no exception, least of all in this last decade.

Below: Elevated Walkways — The Campus Umbilical Cords

The Fourth Chancellor
(not counting acting and interim stand-ins!)

The decision of Clinton Jones, after nine years as Chancellor, to return to teaching as a member of the Political Science Department was the occasion for Larry Kugler, long-time Dean of the College of Arts and Sciences, to step in as Acting Chancellor for the academic year, 1993-94. This brief interregnum preceded the appointment of Charlie Nelms, most recently Chancellor at Indiana University–Richmond, who took over in September of 1994.

That next academic year (1994-1995) was, in many ways, an unsettling one. If it could be said that there was a "honeymoon period" for the new administration, it did not last for very long. By the time the second semester was under way budget problems, staff lay-offs, a different administrative style in the Office of the Chancellor, and differing perceptions as to campus priorities were the source of renewed tension and uncertainty.

These problems were exacerbated and at least in one case underscored by the resignations of three key campus administrators. Victor Wong, for nine years Provost, decided to pursue his interests in spin physics by way of a research grant and an appointment in Ann Arbor; Jacqueline Zeff, Dean of the College of Arts and Sciences, announced her decision to return to teaching as a professor in the English Department. Her decision, apparently, proceeded from a perception of "matters of principle," including issues relating to the CAS budget. And, finally, Steve Hallam, Dean of the School of Management, left to accept an appointment at the University of Akron.

Each of these positions was filled with an interim appointment: Kathy Lavoie in the College of Arts and Sciences; Rodney McGraw in the School of Management; and — who else? — Larry Kugler in the Office of the Provost. None have matched his range of administrative experience on the Flint Campus. Larry Kugler had been Chair of the Mathematics Department, Dean of the College of Arts and Sciences, and then Acting Chancellor prior to his appointment as Interim Provost. Only Wes Rae had come close. At one time or another he had been Chair of the English Department, Dean of the College of Arts and Sciences, and — for a time while Dean — the Acting Provost. Another vertical climb, of course, had been that of Joe Roberson whose varied career has already been described.

There were two themes evident in this recent past, i.e. in 1994-96. First, faculty and staff were even more inclined to define their place, their "community," in relation to the department, area, or office where they were located. It had become a sense of place and of belonging rather narrowly defined. This was the small group that shared some immediately evident common professional and work interests, drank coffee together, gossiped together, and, when things went well, had shared a sense of camaraderie. Others found that "community" among professional colleagues at other institutions, connections that were often maintained via e-mail. A minority of faculty were engaged in committee work and program initiatives that, in a consistent and significant way, involved them in the larger campus community.

For many of the Flint faculty, that larger sense of community — the campus community — was increasingly only a remote abstraction. One senior faculty member, commenting on this development, remarked that "ten years ago (or maybe longer than that) faculty had a more proprietary view of the campus." She went on to say that "many people then took the broad view and felt some responsibility for shaping the future . . . now people tend to assume that their fate is in someone else's hands . . . and just look to protect their own little turf." What was being suggested was that unless administrative policy and decision had some immediately identifiable consequence for one's own "turf," most faculty in more recent years were far less inclined to get involved than had been the case in earlier years. A sense of proprietorship is a helpful way to phrase the issue.

It's fascinating to ponder this emerging campus faculty phenomenon as a kind of microcosm of what has happened to the sense of community in American society in recent decades. In both cases there has been fragmentation. The causes are not at all immediately self-evident. The effects of a self-focused individualism? A sense of alienation from "those in charge"? A sense of disempowerment and isolation in an environment increasingly impersonal and bureaucratic? A sense of divergent values and priorities? For some, certainly, the cause was at least first of all more immediate and personal. It was first of all a sense of overload from the demands of teaching, professional commitments, institutional work, and family obligations.

The second theme had to do with the larger issues, a campus agenda set forth by Chancellor Nelms. Apart from the administration and some of the staff it is difficult to assess how fully engaged students and faculty were in the development and pursuit of that campus agenda.

Among the more important priorities identified by Charlie Nelms were opening the lines of communication on the campus ("dialogue" was the word!), the development of an academic plan, the development of an enrollment management strategy, and a refinement of the budget process. For the new Chancellor, the common denominator of this agenda was "a more student centered" campus.

Budget "refinement" came to mean doing something about contingency funding by moving toward base funding, assuring accountability, making decisions about budget reallocations, and — for some — having to face layoffs. The campus has had several experiences with "RIF's," as they were called. "Reduction-in-Force" decisions, or lay-offs, which always seemed to be handled ineptly and which were talked about for some months before actual personnel decisions were made, invariably had serious morale consequences among the staff, going well beyond those most immediately affected. More than a few staff have asked if these budget decisions, which have such serious impact on the lives of loyal staff, might be handled more humanely and equitably.

While budget matters occupied a good deal of energy and time that first year, the issues of enrollment management and academic planning likely had the more enduring consequences. (The obvious exception being the circumstances of those persons laid off!)

Under the direction of Virginia Allen, the new Vice Chancellor for Student Services and Enrollment Management, strategies were developed with emphases on "student retention, recruitment, and marketing." It was intended that everyone — administrators, faculty, and staff — would be engaged in the effort to attract and retain more students, in assuring a more "user-friendly campus environment," and in assuring that the campus became "more student centered."

In this regard it was a bit more than an irony — it was a contradiction — that budget reallocations were to bring to a virtual end the Student Health Service, a student service in existence for more than two decades! One wonders how this decision was presumed to be "student-centered!" At least two thousand students each year had reason to avail themselves of the Student Health Service. It had been one of the busiest, most used "services" in Student Services. Other decisions, among them an information center, better campus "signage," a promise of improved computer support, and some new financial aid procedures, were more convincing illustrations of the new administration's commitment "to treat students better."

The Kugler Academic Plan

The task of developing an academic plan was assigned to a committee appointed by the Chancellor. Larry Kugler chaired the committee that in 1994-95 undertook to rewrite the Mission Statement and address seven "planning clusters" that had been identified by the Chancellor. Those seven included academic quality, campus collaboration, academic programs, minority attainment, community outreach, technology, and student support. It was a charge somewhat narrower in scope than earlier strategic planning efforts. The Kugler Committee was concerned only with academic planning, though its recommendations were to reach over into collateral areas. Earlier plans and reports (Dorr, 1955; Haber, 1969; Vasse, 1974; and Gluck, 1989) had more expansive, campus-wide dimensions.

However more focused the *Kugler Academic Plan* of 1995, both its content and its reception are useful indicators of both continuity (the persistence of tradition) and discontinuity (evidence of new departures, new directions) for the campus. Comparisons with earlier planning efforts, even though the context for those was more expansive, are similarly useful.

The committee's report was intended, apparently, to serve as the basic guide — the strategic academic plan — for The University of Michigan–Flint into the next century. How well it will serve that purpose ultimately must be left to others, at a later time, to determine. Some faculty questioned how seriously this academic plan would be regarded in the years ahead, by either the administration or the faculty! Skeptics suggested the academic plan would have less rather than more to do with developments in academic areas in the years ahead. Others suggested that the results of the committee's work indicated not so much where the institution was headed as where it had found itself at that particular time. Nevertheless the Chancellor was quick to announce, on the occasion of the Regents' meeting on the Flint Campus in September of 1994, that $500,000 had been earmarked to begin implementing some changes immediately. The money was interest accrued from an academic excellence endowment fund established in the late 1970s.

The 1995 Mission Statement had several new emphases not found in earlier documents. The revealing verb in the most recent Mission Statement, perhaps, is "invested." The statement that "The community is invested in our University, and together we work to enhance the cultural, economic, intellectual, and social vitality of the city and region" conveys a different tone and focus than found in earlier mission statements. Arguably this statement implied a much more specifically engaged campus-community relationship than is found in earlier documents with their more general reference to "partnership" and to the campus being an "urban arm" of The University of Michigan with responsibilities appropriate to a regional and urban campus.

The 1995 statement also put forward the startling assertion that "The mission of the University of Michigan–Flint is to be the leading university in our region. . . ." This was viewed by some faculty as "not quite the point that needs to be made" and as "a bit parochial"!! Earlier documents had simply assumed that regional leadership proceeded from the very fact of a regional campus of The University of Michigan in Flint and suggested instead that comparisons of quality and leadership should be with comparable regional campuses of major universities elsewhere around the country. Others concurred in the Chancellor's public statement that "The University of Michigan–Flint, with an emphasis on academic excellence, responsiveness to its students and outreach to the community, will become the university of choice in mid-Michigan." These were not necessarily contradictory views, but they were two quite different ways of looking at the issue.

Elsewhere the 1995 Mission Statement reaffirmed the traditions and principles of a University of Michigan education: critical thinking, humanistic and scientific inquiry, literacy, human and cultural diversity, high quality scholarship, professional accomplishment, and an institutional relevance assured by way of collaboration with local and regional educational institutions. On these matters it was consistent with earlier mission statements.

With regard to the general recommendations found in this academic plan, what was surprising was that they contained very little that was specific. Apart from the recommendation that new graduate programs be considered in "education, health areas and science and mathematics," the plan contained almost nothing concerning program development and new initiatives in undergraduate education. Only a few sentences addressed program development possibilities for undergraduates. Equally, there was only a brief (though certainly important) comment about the unrealized potential of the Office of Extension and Continuing Education and the University's continuing education efforts in the community.

These are perhaps the principal reasons why few faculty raised questions or objections to the content of the academic plan: there was nothing there that appeared threatening or challenging. That was the observation of several faculty. Two members of the planning committee, when asked, explained that the decision had been made rather early not to engage in the kind of planning that would address specific undergraduate program development. That, it was said, would be "best left to the departments and instructional units."

Still, there were those left wondering what the value could be of an "academic plan" if little other than a few generalities were included about undergraduate program development strategies for the years ahead. And there were questions that went beyond curricular matters. Some wondered, for example, why nothing had been proposed in the Plan about the ratio of full-time to part-time instructors — an increasingly serious problem from the point of view of many faculty. Others wondered why the matter of student housing had not arisen. A number of faculty (and staff) for years had believed that a percentage of the student body resident on campus would have a significantly positive effect on the quality of academic life in particular, and campus life in general. Others wondered why there was so little about new program initiatives, or about priorities in undergraduate program development. And, a concern for at least a few others, no mention could be found in the plan of the possibility of student or faculty exchange programs, or of a visiting scholars program.

What the 1995 Academic Plan did include was a set of rather broadly written recommendations that addressed such matters as "assessment of student outcomes," "academic program review," a "wider range of articulated agreements with community colleges and GMI," some new working relationships with Flint and Genesee County schools, closer collaboration with the Flint community, and "increased priority to recruitment of students from Flint and Genesee County. . . ."

The sometimes seemingly singular emphasis on Flint and Genesee County is curious because, increasingly, students were coming from areas of more recent and rapid population growth — for example, south towards Clarkston and east towards Imlay City. Significant growth was occurring in the outer reaches of Genesee County and in the counties beyond. A declining percentage of students was coming from Flint schools, a development which constituted a reversal of enrollment trends from earlier decades. Information to this effect was found in the Plan, a fact which led some faculty to wonder why Flint and Genesee County student recruitment was given such high priority.

It was not surprising, therefore, that some faculty expressed concern that the "vision" of the academic plan should have been more geographically expansive. By the 1990s, of course, it was commonplace to remark that The University of Michigan–Flint was neither singularly Flint- and urban-defined nor was it singularly defined by the larger regional area. It was, in fact, both! The Kugler Plan had reiterated that point, but because of its apparent emphasis on Flint and Genesee County, some questioned whether the plan was an appropriate and balanced response to the emerging demographic realities of the University's expanded service area. As a step in that direction, it should be said that off-site classes, possibly in the Port Huron area, Livingston County and northern Oakland County, were proposed.

Several faculty pointed out that "distance learning" and "interactive learning" by way of computers, videos, and live two-way transmissions would, in any event, gradually diminish the current preoccupation with the urban and regionally defined service areas. Constituencies that defy limited geographic areas will become increasingly important. However, no one thinks that remote classroom sites elsewhere in Michigan, or perhaps someday outside the state, will ever supplant in importance the core of east central Michigan students attending classes and completing a large part of their degree programs at the Riverfront Campus.

Other recommendations found in the plan addressed the continuing need to "recruit and retain minority faculty, staff, and students," to promote an environment supportive of "cultural and human diversity," and to provide students with a "seamless web of friendly services" within a framework of "greater faculty and staff cooperation." Each stands as an important point in the plan. Mention is made, too, of faculty research support, resources for staff development, and increased support for a wide range of technological services. Most of these recommendations, or ones very similar, had found a place in earlier planning documents. It remains to be seen how the campus will proceed differently than in the past.

Whither Quality?

Beyond such recommendations, the committee gave consideration to that apparently elusive matter of "quality." Some faculty found this discussion not quite to the point. Many of the considerations mentioned appeared to fall into the category of necessary *conditions* for attaining quality, but not as useful means for defining quality, of coming to an understanding of the meaning of quality in an institution of higher learning.

The accessibility of faculty, computer support, a sense of academic community, a low student-faculty ratio, physical facilities, and the range of academic and non-academic programs were identified as some of the "areas of quality." These have long been the concern of faculty and of administrators sensitive to the needs of a healthy academic community. Such concerns bear repetition! Better, though, if they had been identified as conditions necessary if high quality is to be attained rather than as elements in a definition of quality.

Closer to the point, perhaps, the committee noted that "quality requires . . . ongoing evaluation of the effectiveness of our programs and support services: are they doing what we want them to do?" To some it appeared that only in the last two sentences of this section was the issue of quality clearly addressed. Those sentences read: "One very important measure of quality for UM–Flint is assessment of student outcomes. Because student learning is central to the UM–Flint mission, how students are changed during their UM–Flint experience is of utmost importance."

"Quality," some faculty were to point out, ultimately is a measure and judgment about intellectual, moral, and professional growth and maturity. Quality measures those dimensions of the total person that universities are best equipped to address, such as intellectual acumen, acquired knowledge, a range of defined skills, and a level of literacy. It is the measure and the judgment that are important. Most faculty appear to believe that they have a rather clear, although subjective, understanding of what is meant in a university setting by standards and measures of "quality." Generally it is an understanding derived from experiences elsewhere, or from knowledge about other places. It derives from one's cumulative collegial experience. An awareness of expectations from both students and faculty and of "standards" at the "best" colleges and universities around the country have been instrumental in forming those understandings. While quality and excellence are difficult to define, listening to faculty talk about their courses, their seminars, their laboratories, and, most of all, the expectations they have of the very best of their students gives those words meaning.

Quality can also be considered from the vantage point of those developments by which it is diminished. No one is more aware than a faculty member of the consequences of such developments as shorter reading lists in course syllabi, or of grade inflation — the tendency over time to give students better grades than the quality of work might warrant, or of making course and degree expectations less difficult and rigorous. Looked at from this other, negative end, that is what standards and expectations are all about and how faculty, at least, come to regard varying degrees of academic quality.

The faculty appeared to concur with the committee's conclusion that it is the measure and the judgment that requires appreciation and understanding. While the conditions necessary for "quality" and "excellence" are indispensable, it is the measure of change, the assessment of outcomes, by which people are said to have attained a certain standard of accomplishment. The standards themselves should be a matter of continuing concern for the faculty. In practical terms, the credibility of the degree earned is at stake. In a more expansive and fundamental sense, the credibility of the student's education is at stake! Everyone seems to understand that the image and reputation of an institution rests on its ability to maintain and even enhance "quality" and "standards of excellence" in demonstrable ways. What is important is that these words don't simply become empty rhetoric or educationist jargon.

The committee did in fact conclude that "assessment" was the key and proposed the establishment of the means by which both student outcomes assessment and academic program review would be assured.

The reception of the 1995 academic planning venture was mixed. Some, among the faculty at least, thought it quite good and were inclined to speak well of the committee's accomplishment. "Highly commendable!" was the enthusiastic endorsement of one senior faculty member. Others had reservations. One faculty member perhaps summed up the feelings of many of those "others" with the observation that "Academic planning documents should be at least a bit visionary. They should contain those elements that suggest the academic community is setting its sights high, and even taking a few risks. This planning document suggests very little of that — it's too reflective, a bit parochial, and is focused on the immediate moment — not the future."

Whither Liberal Education?

A question not explicitly faced in any mid-1990s planning document or formal discussion was the future place of liberal education, of the arts and sciences, in the ever-widening array of programs offered under the aegis of Academic Affairs. It was increasingly evident that programs that had a clear pre-professional, professional and career emphasis — those with an applied dimension — were more likely to have better access to limited resources.

For many years it was said of The University of Michigan–Flint that its academic programs were rooted and centered in the liberal arts and sciences. That rhetoric by 1995 was muted; in fact it was seldom expressed. The assumption by the mid-1990s, apparently, was that the College of Arts and Sciences, its programs and its faculty, constituted just one of several units in Academic Affairs. The liberal arts were no longer perceived as the center toward which everything else in academic affairs was somehow connected. The image expressed by Chancellor Conny Nelson in the early 1980s, of a flower with its center and its petals radiating out from the center, no longer appeared appropriate. Other values and priorities had moved to the forefront. The consideration being given to the creation of a School of Applied Sciences was symptomatic of new directions and of new priorities.

Whether or not this was the wisest and most appropriate direction in which the University should move was one question. That it should happen willy-nilly without much faculty thought or discussion being given to what will likely emerge as quite a different kind of university was quite another! Faculty grumbling about perceived new directions and emphases has been no substitute for open, purposeful, and reasoned discussion.

It was, of course, all quite deliberate — at least for those who make decisions. Decisions were being made all the time about resource allocation, about how best to be responsive to the needs of the varied constituencies served by the campus, and, on occasion, about choices between the requests from programs in the arts and sciences and those from programs in applied and career areas.

We should not assume from any of this that the arts and the sciences had found themselves in deep trouble. Most of the programs and faculty in the College of Arts and Sciences have flourished and continue to demonstrate promise of even greater things in the future. We might look, for example, at one dimension of this — one that brings the community to the University, and the University to the community.

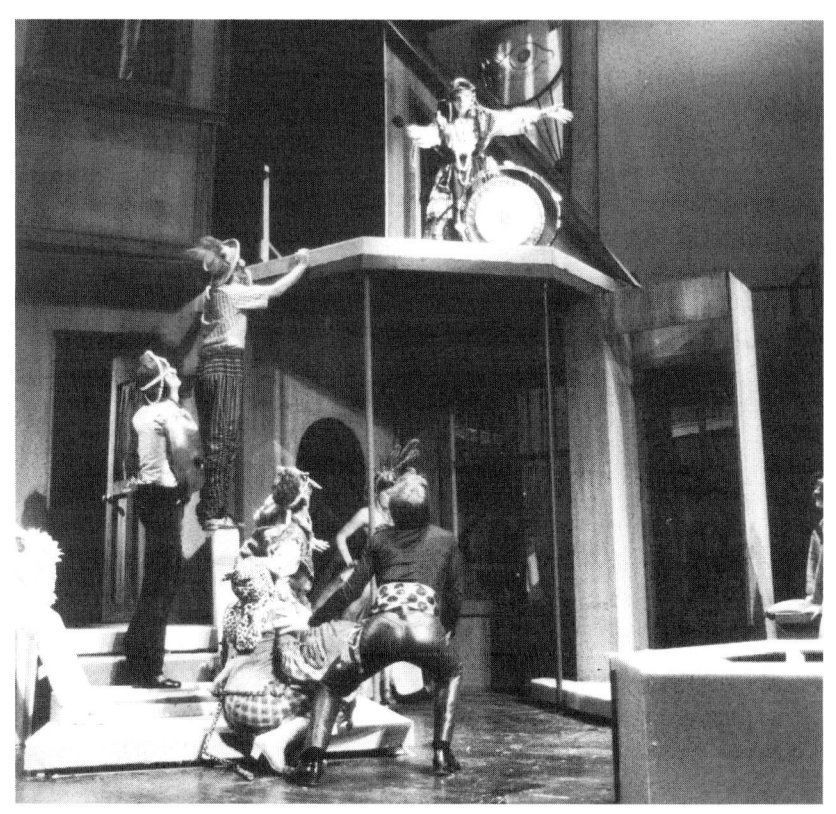

Theatre Production - "Camino Real" — Tennessee Williams

Professor Ray Roth Conducting — Campus Concert

The Arts

A very important and highly visible aspect of The University of Michigan–Flint presence in the community is evident in the arts. As we noted in the first pages of this "portrait," Flint had established itself as an important regional cultural center no later than the end of the nineteenth century. This reputation has been maintained and enhanced by various institutions and organizations that comprise Flint's Cultural Center, most notably the Flint Symphony Orchestra, Bower Theater, the Flint Insititute of Music, the De Waters Art Institute, and the Sloan Museum.

With the passing of each year, the contributions of The University of Michigan–Flint to the community's "arts scene" have become increasingly more prominent and significant. In the 1994-95 academic year, for example, 7,011 people attended 24 performances of four major Theatre Department productions. Numbers of these productions over the years have qualified for submission to the American College Theater Festival. The quality of these productions compares favorably with theater department productions anywhere in Michigan, or beyond.

Music Department concerts and performances, in that same year, were attended by over 4,000 people. Concerts on and off campus have involved an extraordinary array of musical groups: the University Chorale, Chamber Singers, Vocal Jazz Ensemble, Jazz Combo, Jazz Band, University Band, Percussion Ensemble, Saxophone Quartet, Contemporary Music Ensemble, Flute Choir, Brass Quintet, and a Tuba Ensemble. That's a dozen groups that bring exciting music to the Flint area.

In that same year four performances in the Spotlight Series drew an audience of 1,540. The four lectures that were part of the Critical Issues Forum were attended by 1,200. Not the least, the University's television station, WFUM/TV28, broadcast to 183,000 households each week. That marked a 47% increase from 1991.

Poetry readings, art exhibits, dance performances, and special lectures by faculty to a wide range of community organizations and groups added yet other dimensions to the University's cultural and artistic role in the community. For the arts and sciences faculty, cultural and artistic involvement in the community provides great opportunities to bring to the area a wide array of intellectual and artistic talent and achievement.

So, at the very least, the arts and sciences are quite well and very much alive in an environment where career, applied, and professional programs seem to be favored — for the moment, at least. In the future much will depend on the effectiveness of the College of Arts and Sciences Dean, Executive Committee and Council of Chairs in two areas: securing resources and insisting on the centrality of a liberal education in the mission of The University of Michigan–Flint. Equally important will be the presence of an articulate, informed and credible faculty leadership.

Conclusion and Comment

A portrait of "a Work in Progress" is difficult to conclude. In fact, the very phrase "in progress" suggests that The University of Michigan–Flint has yet to attain a firm threshold definition, a defined personality, and a clear sense of self as a regional campus. That should not be surprising. Only a little more than two decades have passed since the Flint College became a regional university campus of The University of Michigan.

It is more than likely true that had the Flint Campus developed as an altogether separate state university a more clearly defined institutional identity would have already emerged. A continuing task for the Flint Campus has been how to be The University of Michigan in Flint — a campus with its own established identity, and yet an identity that clearly reflects the fact it is equally an integral part of The University of Michigan system. Significant progress has been made toward securing that identity, but it is not yet a finished task. Mission statements, strategic plans, and public statements by campus administrators are sometimes helpful but they fall short of what is ultimately required. When faculty, students, and staff become aware of a developed sense of campus community and what it means to be "Michigan" in Flint, then that threshold will have been attained.

There are certain advantages to being on this side of the threshold, on this side of a clear and established sense of institutional identity, of what it really means to be a part of The University of Michigan–Flint community. In any institution that has not yet been fully formed and defined there are greater opportunities for the innovative and for the experimental, greater opportunities to link the visionary with the practical, and, with luck, to encourage thinking to move in unorthodox and even radical directions. Those are the proper responsibilities of universities.

As many faculty have observed over the past nearly four decades, this circumstance, this freedom from the constraints of well established patterns, has been one of the most attractive features of the Flint Campus. To the extent that a more open, fluid academic environment does indeed continue to prevail, then the opportunities exist for thinking differently about some very fundamental matters.

Some New Thinking

Examples abound — in program and course development, the application of new technologies, and in ideas about the nature of learning. One hopes, for example, that generally accepted understandings about learning, at the Flint Campus and elsewhere, will be re-examined. One also hopes that the whole process of education will become more encompassing, more holistic. This means that higher education needs to include but at the same time reach beyond the rigorous disciplines of analytical and empirical thinking. It also needs to encompass and at the same time reach beyond traditional approaches to aesthetic appreciation.

It seems clear that increasingly over the past five hundred years education in the Western world has focused on the principal activities of the "left" hemisphere of the brain. We can only expand our awareness and deepen our humanity if due regard is given to the potential of the largely neglected "right" hemisphere of the brain. Or, for those who prefer the more precise language of neural science, the connections between the amygdala (and related limbic structures) and the neocortex — which is to say, between the head and the heart, between thinking and feeling.

In a too often misunderstood phrase, education needs to be more "spirit-centered." It needs to help students acquire a wider field of awareness. In that overworked contemporary expression, it needs to become more "holistic."

By spirit-centered we mean a process of disciplined learning that encompasses more of those dimensions of the human spirit that are expressed in large part by the *intuitive* and *imaginative* capacities of the human mind. We also mean an education that pays more attention to questions of meaning, purpose, and moral values. The idea of "the human spirit" and of "the spiritual," as well as concerns about meaning, have too often been simply dismissed as falling more appropriately within the realm of those traditions and institutions that are founded on specific systems of belief. We need to recognize that the full dimensions of the human spirit are the proper domain of higher education.

Attention to the different ways in which we come to know and understand the world, to the different ways in which we experience the world, and to the wider arena of human *awareness* can only enrich and deepen education. Arguably, higher education should pay greater heed to the full dimensions of what it means to be human, and to the wider scope of learning. There have always been those faculty, of course, who have been sensitive to these concerns. The number needs to increase and reach beyond just a few courses to include much of what the varied academic programs of the several schools and colleges are about.

Much of higher education for a long time has had a narrower focus. With the pervasive influence of a positivist tradition that has roots in the nineteenth century, a tradition which has given disproportionate influence to quantifiable data and empirically verifiable cause-effect experience, higher education has largely failed to fully nurture the other ways in which human beings can grow, learn, and search for truth.

This more expansive, encompassing approach to learning, of course, assumes that at the same time a better job can be done with the more traditional agenda in higher education: quantitative skills, writing skills, and the other principal elements of what has come to be regarded as a liberal education. This assumes rigor in analytical and empirical thinking. It also assumes that professional and pre-professional programs will carefully monitor what students are actually learning and, with everyone else, think more expansively about "outcomes assessment." Thinking more expansively will go beyond concerns about the traditional norms of rigor and quality; it will proceed from new ideas about what learning and education entail.

A more holistic approach to learning, one wherein learning and the search for truth are valued in their own right and not as a means to an end, will envisage and engage whole new paradigms about thinking and feeling, about relationships, politics, society, the environment, nature, resources, and meaning. It will be one that can fully embrace the Information Age. It will place the Information Age within an appropriately human as opposed to a technological and scientific context. It will be one that will allow human beings to better understand themselves — their place in the world and in the cosmos — in ways far more expansive than those that have largely prevailed in the Western world for the past five centuries.

There are many aspects to these new challenges, some of which address other matters than intuition and imagination, questions of meaning and of the human spirit, or even thinking about learning from a more holistic perspective.

There are those who would dismiss many of these ideas as either irrelevant or as inappropriate in today's essentially scientific and technological world. There are yet others who regard traditional statements about liberal education as anachronistic, as perceptions or values appropriate only to another time. But beyond those individuals there are others who express a wide range of legitimate opinion, certainly, the substance of which is essential to constructive debate about the purposes and content of higher education. What must be pursued, with greater energy, is the debate.

In that debate we need to be reminded, once again, of the concerns expressed a quarter of a century ago by the sociologist, Robert Nisbet. In the early 1970s Nisbet warned that universities were drifting away from "the rational, dispassionate search for truth," that central commitment which has sustained universities for centuries. Instead, there emerged a growing eagerness to redress social ills as the first order of business: an agenda of racial, ethnic, gender, class and economic issues, an agenda which very quickly went far beyond the need for universities to become more inclusive and responsive. In its extreme form this new commitment is expressed by way of a postmodernist relativism that denigrates traditional ideals of intellectual discipline and derides ideas of truth, knowledge, and objectivity. In its most evident and current form it gives priority to the immediately utilitarian. It almost always leads to a confusion of means and ends as universities articulate goal and mission statements. And it clearly has diminished the traditions and ideals of a liberal education.

About Community Expectations . . .

Arguably, the best of what higher education has been, its traditional purposes, deserves renewed attention and commitment in order that those ideals may be assured a place as distinguishing and central characteristics of higher education in the future.

The eminent American historian, Henry Steele Commager, identified that central dimension of the purposes of higher education when he remarked that,

> "The University is the only institution in Western society whose business is to search for and transmit truth regardless of all competing or conflicting pressures and demands: pressures for immediate usefulness, for social approval, pressures to serve the special interests of government, a class, a professional group, a race, a faith, even a nation."

In an age of "political correctness" and utilitarian education this has become a radical statement. It is not a statement likely to generate enthusiasm in a community where the university is seen as a principal resource by means of which a range of social, economic and other interests are served and problems solved. The immediate usefulness of the university has come to be assumed as a matter of simple fact by local and area business and other interests.

The problem is that colleges and universities too often have allowed their purpose and usefulness to be defined by the immediate needs of particular groups and interests. Further, they are encouraged to become career training centers. This is now not only perceived as the practical strategy; it is viewed as politically necessary, as a simple fact of survival. Some, of course, see nothing wrong with this. It is simply a matter of assuring that the "ivory tower" becomes relevant and responsive in the modern world. It assures that academia will be accountable.

Others, and there may be more of us as time passes, have concluded that the best of what relevance, accountability and even partnership convey is truly secured only when the larger community recognizes that its own best, long-term interests are served when the university is allowed, even encouraged, to be first of all true to its highest and most important mission: the pursuit of truth. In being able to do so an academic community is less likely to confuse ends and means. For example, the pursuit of diversity and minority initiatives, or of projects in applied research of interest to that community, thereby become the means by which academic excellence is secured and truth pursued, and not simply as ends in themselves. Both the academic community and the society it serves — its constituencies — gain in this kind of mutually trusting and supportive relationship.

We might recall that the *Dorr Report,* by which The University of Michigan's Flint College was established in 1956, conveyed precisely this kind of mutual understanding and trust between the people of the City of Flint and the University. Times and circumstances indeed have changed, but perhaps that change can be best accommodated by a recovery and reaffirmation of this very central idea from the past.

By the early 1990s, if not some years earlier, there was a growing feeling that The University of Michigan–Flint had a special and perhaps central role in assuring the economic development and well-being of the Flint area. Such assumptions, within the framework of a university-community partnership, have been and remain unfortunate. Care has been needed to assure that the important difference between being a "resource" and being an agency engaged in the tasks of revitalization and growth is understood. Occasional community comment about the role of both PURA (the Project for Urban and Regional Affairs) and CSR (the Community Stabilization and Revitalization Project) — which are the major outreach programs of the university — suggest at least some confusion on this point. Flint, Genesee County, and the surrounding region should not come to regard The University of Michigan–Flint largely as an instrument by means of which downtown revitalization and regional economic development and diversification occur. Misunderstanding and problems arise when there are inappropriate community expectations — or university expectations, for that matter.

There are other aspects to this matter of expectations. The University should not allow itself to come to be viewed as the means by which students, after completing a series of prescribed course requirements and accumulating the requisite number of credit hours, are then "degreed and credentialed." That's putting the matter rather baldly, but it is becoming a problem, one based upon increasingly evident attitudes and expectations.

This is not to say that the University is not a resource for the community or that its credit hours, course sequences and degrees are unimportant. Rather, the nature and role of that resource and the meaning of those degrees and credit hours need to be understood in relation to the priority goals and purposes of higher education. There is the danger of those understandings being overlooked or dismissed.

The partnership of the university and the communities and populations it serves should be clearly understood. Students should understand, as some do not, that the goal is that of an education; the degree is simply an acknowledgement of that education, itself, in a very real sense, indicative only of a "work in progress." That sounds self evident. All too often both the concept of partnership and the purposes of education are no longer either self evident or clearly understood.

The Corporate Model — Running it like a Business?

It seems increasingly evident that, over the past quarter of a century, universities have come to set themselves up with an eye to the corporate model, with the president or the chancellor running these places as though they were businesses. And like the concerns of the CEO of a business enterprise, the primary concerns of university officials have become those of "the bottom line" — enrollments, marketing, advertising, total quality management strategies, leadership teams, costs per student credit hour, head counts, retention rates, and various other aspects of what is really a rather narrow perspective on accountability. One faculty member was overheard remarking that this focus has turned everyone into "just bean counters."

While budgetary matters are clearly important, cannot one reasonably ask where teaching, learning, indeed education, fit into this hierarchy of corporate business priorities and values? Surely an organizational model more appropriate to learning, to a faculty-student centered enterprise, could be found. More than likely, those models do exist and can be found scattered about in higher education. It might be advisable for both administrative and faculty leadership to look about.

Accountability includes but should go well beyond simple dollars. Indeed, accountability needs to *begin* with other concerns than with dollars. It needs to *begin* with truly educated students, equipped with the skills, knowledge, and moral and aesthetic sensitivity to live responsibly and creatively in the larger world; it needs to *begin* with the "outcomes assessment" concerns expressed in the Kugler Academic Plan; it needs to *begin* with a talented faculty committed to excellence in teaching and professional accomplishment — a faculty fully engaged in the learning enterprise.

These should be the first two points of accountability: the students, and the faculty — the measure of who they are, what they are doing, and what they are accomplishing. When this priority is clearly established and acted on, then an appropriate organizational model, with all of the necessary administrative policy, procedure, and rhetoric, could then fall in place. Maybe then market strategies, total quality management, head counts and retention rates, advertising schemes, and decision making procedures that diminish shared governance will all be set aside for concerns and values more appropriate to the central tasks of higher education. Maybe then the interests of faculty and students engaged in learning will be at the top and center of administrative concerns. The practical matters of administrative responsibility, however obviously important and urgent, thereby become the necessary means and not the evident ends of what they, the administrators, are about. Only then does accountability acquire appropriate meaning.

Administrators in higher education need first to be educators who truly understand and appreciate the scholarship, teaching, and academic values appropriate to truly good universities. They need, themselves, to be men and women of scholarly attainment and significant academic experience. All of the administrative skills are clearly and obviously important, but they should be secondary. Otherwise it's not very long before there is confusion and doubt as to mission, purposes, and goals. Priorities are turned upside down. The central idea of what a university should be about risks being compromised.

The unease so evident in colleges and universities across the country, signs of structural difficulty in the ways in which institutions of higher learning are organized, the sense that higher education is seriously falling short of the expectations society has for it, concerns about the real value of the baccalaureate degree, and the evident worry about articulating mission and goal statements and responding to concerns about academic quality all may be the gray before the dawn. They may be the signs of the academic community beginning to experience renewal and transformation. We can hope so!

Room for Optimism

There is room for optimism. When asked what she thought about the current "health" of The University of Michigan–Flint, on a scale of one to ten, one senior faculty member, looking very somber, said "Six", and then, with a broad smile, added ". . . and improving!" In the larger and more expansive sense of things, many on the Flint Campus would concur. In an altogether unscientific and random sampling among senior faculty in August and September of 1995 — of those who had been around for ten years or more — most responded with numbers ranging from four to six, a few said three, and one generously offered an eight.

One very consistent characteristic about the Flint faculty has been a stubborn and admirable (if inexplicable) optimism. One might wonder why it is, if so much has evidently gone wrong or is amiss, that most faculty over the years have chosen to remain at the Flint Campus. When asked, the responses have ranged from "It's never been boring around here — things are always happening!", to "More often than not, this has been a fun place with interesting people!" Some have said that, beyond it being a good place to teach, they have wanted to stay around long enough to see what happens to the place. And for some of those, that has meant staying for twenty, thirty, or more years. It's also seen as a place where there is room for and tolerance for the new and the different — a place where there is a bit of elbow room to do things differently without getting burned in the process — especially if you've already been granted tenure.

A persistent optimism about the eventual outcome of "a work in progress" seems to characterize most of the faculty in sufficient measure to carry them from one issue and problem to the next. It remains a question as to whether Flint simply attracts this kind of faculty, or whether they undergo some kind of attitudinal metamorphosis once here.

The tasks of renewal and transformation are in no way simple nor are they without difficulty. In all likelihood those tasks go beyond the rhetoric and particulars of mission statements and strategic planning documents. Success will likely require new thinking by faculty, students, staff, and administrators. It may require the infusion of new talent, of some new faces that will bring new perspectives and energy to these tasks. Many think so!

One particular perspective is required. To know where you are and where you are going, it's well to know where you have been, in this instance to have in mind the story of The University of Michigan–Flint. That, in just a few words, is the value of a historical perspective. To have a compelling vision of the future requires a sense of the past as well as an awareness of future possibilities, of tomorrow's opportunities. It's important that both aspects of this perspective are appreciated. The two go together.

Equally important, the communities and interests served by the University should come to better understand the special, even unique, place required by the University in order that those interests and needs may be well served and to enable The University of Michigan–Flint to become a truly distinguished institution. The development of that understanding will be a principal task for the campus community — especially faculty, administrators, and the alumni.

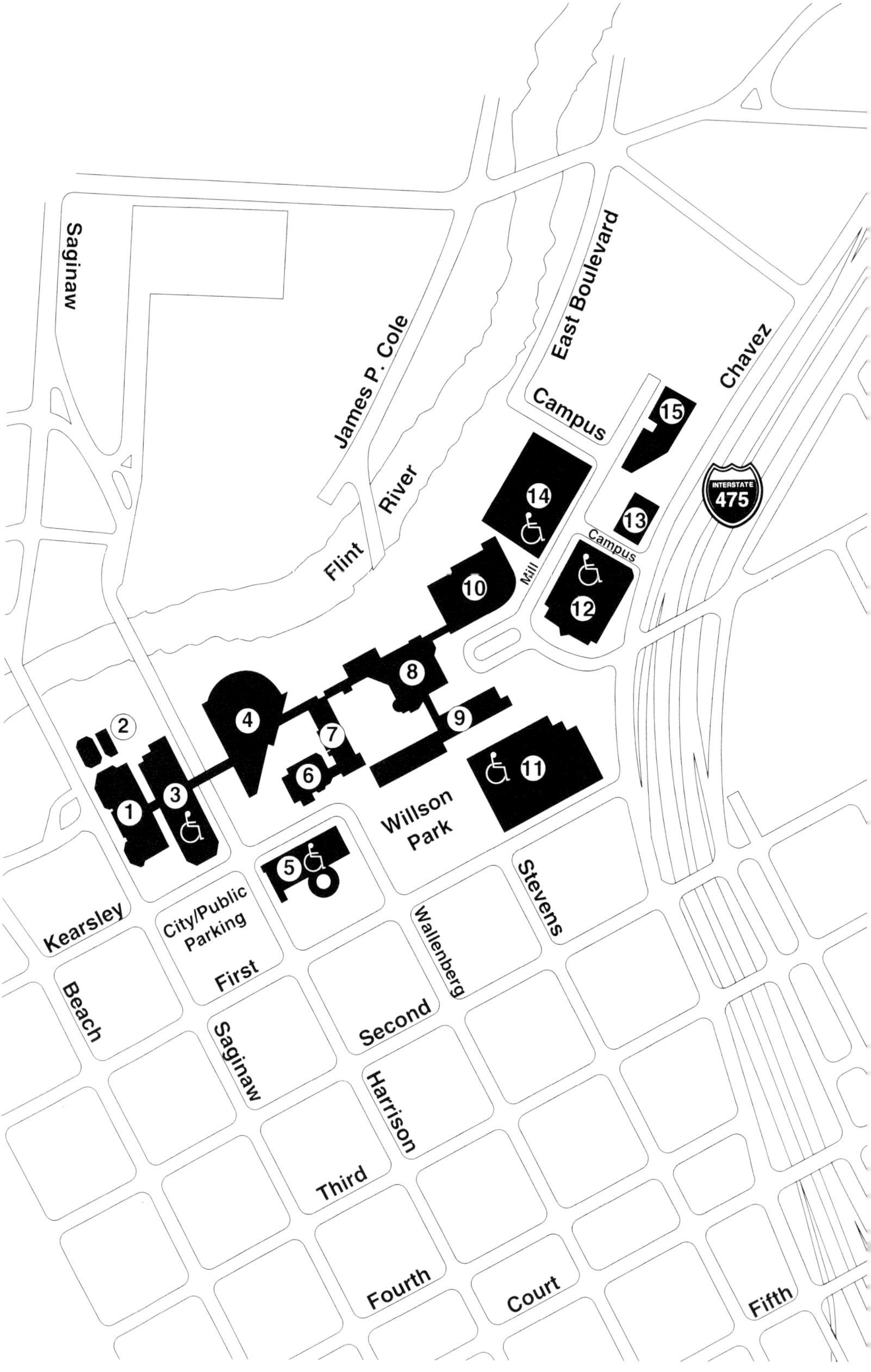
Saginaw
James P. Cole
East Boulevard
Chavez
Campus
15
14
13
INTERSTATE
475
Campus
Mill
Flint
River
10
12
8
4
2
7
9
3
1
6
11
Willson
Park
5
Kearsley
City/Public
Parking
Stevens
Wallenberg
First
Beach
Second
Saginaw
Harrison
Third
Fourth
Court
Fifth